Napoleon at Bay, 1814

Napoleon at Bay, 1814

The Campaigns to the fall
of the First Empire

F. Loraine Petre

LEONAUR

Napoleon at Bay, 1814
The Campaigns to the fall
of the First Empire

by F. Loraine Petre

First published under the titles
Napoleon at Bay, 1814

Leonaur is an imprint
of Oakpast Ltd

Copyright in this form © 2009 Oakpast Ltd

ISBN: 978-1-84677-738-7 (hardcover)
ISBN: 978-1-84677-737-0 (softcover)

http://www.leonaur.com

Publisher's Notes

In the interests of authenticity, the spellings, grammar and place names
used have been retained from the original editions.

The opinions of the authors represent a view of events in which he
was a participant related from his own perspective,
as such the text is relevant as an historical document.

The views expressed in this book are not necessarily
those of the publisher.

Contents

Author's Preface

This volume will appear almost precisely one hundred years after the commencement of the campaign which it describes. As in the case of the author's four previous histories of Napoleon's campaigns, it deals only with the purely military side of the war, politics being referred to only in so far as they actually influenced directly the course of military operations. Further, it is confined to the operations in which Napoleon was personally and directly engaged.

Therefore, no attempt is made to deal with the campaigns of Soult and Suchet against Wellington, with the blockade of Davout in Hamburg or of the other fortresses in Germany, with Maison's campaign in the Netherlands, with Eugène's in Italy, or even with Augereau's movements about Lyons. The latter, feeble though they were, certainly did exercise a considerable influence on the allied movements, especially in the end of February; but it was mainly unfounded alarm which influenced Schwarzenberg, and the details of Augereau's advance and retreat are of little interest.

There appears to be, at present, no modern work in English giving anything like a full history of this campaign, except the lectures of Captain Jones published in 1868. Being addressed to Sandhurst cadets they necessarily do not go into much detail. When they were delivered, even Napoleon's correspondence was scarcely published in full, and none of the many documents which have since been disinterred from the various record offices of Europe were available.

In French there are several excellent histories, notably the *1814* of the late M. Henry Houssaye, and the admirable volumes of Commandant Weil, which represent the result of years of assiduous search in the archives of Paris, St. Petersburg, and Vienna. Captain Hulot, of the 45th Infantry, has also published a useful volume, *La Manoeuvre de Laon*. In German there are contemporary accounts by Müffling and Clausewitz, and a translation of Danilewski's Russian work, which has also been translated into English. Two volumes (by General Janson) of the great *Geschichte der Befreiungskriege, 1813-1815* deal with 1814. That author naturally had freer access to German records than Colonel Weil, but, save in this respect, little has been added to the French work.

The author has been over the greater part of the theatre of war, and, in the case of the country between Soissons, Laon, and Berry-au-Bac, had the advantage of seeing 10,000 French troops of the present day manoeuvring with general ideas very similar to those of Napoleon of March 7th-9th, 1814. The whole thing was a vivid object-lesson in the difference between the simple training of a few weeks which enabled Napoleon to pit his recruits with success against the veterans of the allied armies, and the far lengthier and stricter training which alone can qualify men to meet the more exacting conditions of warfare in the twentieth century.

F. L. P.

31st October; 1913.

CHAPTER 1

From Hanau to Châlons

Napoleon's campaigns of 1813 and 1814 were in reality a continuation of that of 1812; but the well-marked pauses in the end of 1812 and beginning of 1813, and again in the end of 1813, naturally lead to their treatment as three separate parts. When Napoleon recrossed the Rhine, in the beginning of November, 1813, with the 60,000 or 70,000 soldiers whom alone he had saved from the disaster of Leipzig, the allies lost touch of him for a considerable period. It will be well to describe briefly the general military situation of Europe at this time. Napoleon, with his field army, had been finally driven from Germany; but he had still in that country large garrisons occupying the important fortresses which had not been retaken from him, and which were now isolated in the midst of hostile forces and a hostile population; for the Emperor had no longer any German ally, and the auxiliary forces of Bavaria, Saxony, and the other states of the late Rhenish Confederation were now being led against him, and recruited by fresh levies.

Though some of the garrisons left behind in Germany had to surrender before the end of the campaign, they accounted for a very large force lost to Napoleon. Nearly 100,000 men were in Dresden, Magdeburg, Glogau, Hamburg, Küstrin and Wittenberg alone. He had, moreover, to provide garrisons for the fortresses on the Rhine and in Eastern and Northern France which would soon be surrounded by the rising tide of invasion.

Mayence alone had a garrison of about 15,000 men. There were more fortresses in Belgium and Holland with only a small field army which never exceeded about 15,000 men.

On the Pyreneean frontier Soult, with about 60,000 men, faced Wellington, already over the frontier, and Suchet, with 37,000, was opposed to the Anglo-Spanish forces in the north-east corner of Spain. In Italy, the Viceroy had some 50,000 men against about equal numbers of Austrians under Bellegarde. Murat was for the moment on the French side with the Neapolitan army, but he was already wavering and soon changed sides.

In the campaign which we are about to describe, diplomacy and politics played an unusually important part. With all powers, both military and political, united in his own hands, there was, in Napoleon's case, a constant harmony of operations, though he found himself hampered in his military movements by the necessity of always covering Paris, and of avoiding situations which might give rise to alarm in the capital, and thereby offer opportunities to the many enemies of his government there.

Paris was the heart and centre of his power, the storehouse of his military supplies, and the headquarters of his army organizations. It represented France in a way that Moscow did not represent Russia in 1812 or Berlin Prussia in 1813. At the same time, it was the cauldron in which seethed all the forces of revolution and discontent, and all the intrigues of the parties opposed to the Napoleonic régime. All France, and Paris especially, was weary of the Empire and of the years of war which it had represented. Napoleon knew well that the fall of Paris entailed that of the Empire, and Paris was then not a fortress capable of making a serious resistance whilst the Emperor organized fresh armies south of the Loire.

On the side of the allies, political interests were far more complicated, as is always the case with allied armies. The interests of the several powers were very divergent, and we shall constantly see their military operations very largely ruled by the selfish interests of one or the other.

The Tsar personally cherished the idea of an occupation of

Paris to avenge Napoleon's occupation of Moscow in 1812; but he found himself restrained in this by the strong feeling, dating from before Kutuzow's death in 1813, that Russia had played her part in driving back the French from her own territory with the awful losses of the retreat. Many of his statesmen and commanders saw no sufficient reason, after that, for fighting other people's battles in Central and Western Europe.

Austria, as represented by Metternich and the Emperor, was in a different position. After the successes gained in Germany in 1813, it was practically certain that any peace that could be concluded with Napoleon would end in the restoration to her of practically all she had lost in recent wars. A continuation of the war, and the overthrow of Napoleon, would tend to the increase of the power and influence of her old rivals Russia and Prussia, which she could not regard with satisfaction, especially as Russia was understood to have views as to the disposition of Poland which suited neither Austria nor Prussia. Some weight, not too much, may also be given to the Austrian Emperor's unwillingness to assist in the complete overthrow of his daughter's husband Napoleon.

The King of Prussia, a devoted adherent of the Tsar, was generally ready to follow his lead. On the other hand, the feeling of his subjects, and of many of his statesmen and generals, was one of intense bitterness against the man who had oppressed them for seven years, and of burning desire for revenge against him and his army.

England, weary of protracted war, and of playing paymaster to the Powers of the various coalitions, was ready to welcome peace, provided there were reasonable guarantees for its permanence. The ever-intriguing Bernadotte was another source of trouble; for he had wild visions of himself as the successor of Napoleon, by election of the French people. It is supposed to have been at his instigation that the allies proclaimed that Napoleon, not the French people, was the enemy.

With such divergent views prevailing at head-quarters of the allies it was obvious that compromise must be the order of the day, unless there was to be a break-up of the coalition.

When we come to the military leaders, we find on the one side Napoleon served as subordinates by marshals who, however excellent as corps commanders, were none of them fit for semi-independent command, and moreover, were as tired of war, for the most part, as was the rest of France. They had been liberally endowed by their master, and were now only anxious to enjoy their wealth and honours in peace.

On the side of the allies, the commander-in-chief, Prince Schwarzenberg, by nature a statesman and diplomatist rather than a general, was terribly lacking in enterprise, tormented by a constant fear of attacks on his lines of communication, and intolerably slow in moving. On the other hand, some excuse may be found for him in the difficulties of his position as the servant of many masters. He owed allegiance primarily to his own sovereign the Austrian Emperor and his adviser Metternich, neither of whom favoured bold measures or a vigorous attempt finally to overthrow Napoleon. The Tsar, who had arrogated to himself the principal position among the three sovereigns, and was fond of interfering in military matters, constantly urged Schwarzenberg forward, and even at times passed orders on his own account. The King of Prussia generally followed Alexander.

The commander-in-chief of the army of Silesia, the veteran Blücher, was the very reverse of Schwarzenberg. He hated Napoleon with a bitter hatred; nothing would satisfy him but the Emperor's early and complete downfall. He was all for an immediate advance on Paris, which was not at all what Schwarzenberg or Metternich or the Emperor Francis desired. Yet Blücher was never insubordinate, though it must be admitted that he advocated and rejoiced in separation of the armies as giving him a freer hand. No one has ever accused Blücher of being a heaven-born genius, but he was full of common sense and did not hesitate to rely for brainwork on his more talented subordinate Gneisenau. If Gneisenau supplied the brains, it was Blücher who supplied the relentless energy, the fierce patriotism, and the strong will which pushed his army forward and kept peace between Russians and Prussians, and even between Prussians and Prussians in the campaign about Laon. When Blücher, broken down by fever and ophthalmia at Laon, was compelled to delegate his command temporarily to Gneisenau, the results were immediately apparent in Gneisenau's cancellation of the orders for an immediate pursuit of the defeated French, and in the inactivity of the Silesian army during the days on which Blücher was incapacitated. Blücher undoubtedly was the hero of the campaign on the allied side. But for his energy, it might well have had a different end.

Arrived at Frankfort-on-the-Main, the allies settled down to lengthy deliberations and councils of war. Blücher was all for an immediate continuation of the pursuit of the defeated French army of Leipzig, right up to the gates of Paris. On the 3rd November he wrote through Gneisenau to Knesebeck: [1] "We can now take stock of the position of Napoleon. If we move rapidly on Holland and cross the Rhine, the conquest of Holland will be an accomplished fact in less than two months, and we shall sign a durable peace.

If, on the contrary, we remain on the right bank, if we allow ourselves to be delayed by negotiations, we shall have to engage, in 1814, in a severe and bloody campaign." The writer saw as clearly as did Napoleon himself that the one thing absolutely necessary to the latter was time to reorganize and recruit his army. A fortnight later Napoleon himself expressed the same idea in a letter to Marmont. "We are not, at present, ready for anything. In the first fortnight of January we shall be already prepared for much." [2] Had Blücher's general idea been followed, the Empire of Napoleon would probably have fallen before the end of December.

Clausewitz, in his critical essay on the campaign, has shown that the allies might well have advanced, after a week's rest on

---

1. Knesebeck was the principal military adviser of the King of Prussia. He was thoroughly imbued with the antiquated principles of 18th century war, was all for manoeuvring, and seemed to consider a great battle the last resort of a desperate leader, rather than as the primary objective to be aimed at.
2. *Corr.* 20,921.

the Rhine, with 245,000 men, even after detaching 40,000 men with Bernadotte against Davout in Hamburg. Clausewitz calculates that of the 245,000 a force of 65,000 would have sufficed to mask the eastern fortresses. Deducting another 30,000 for losses in action, by disease, etc., at least 150,000 allies could have arrived before Paris. Napoleon's 60,000 or 70,000 would have dwindled by a number at least as great as the reinforcements he could have gathered in the meanwhile, and, moreover, they would have reached Paris thoroughly demoralized by a continuous retreat of nearly 500 miles after the great defeat of Leipzig. The result of a decisive battle east of Paris, under such circumstances, could hardly be doubtful.

But an immediate advance was not to be expected under the political conditions prevailing at the allied headquarters. On the 9th November commenced a series of councils of war, of plans of campaign, and of tentative negotiations with Napoleon. The allies still offered terms of peace which would have left France with her "natural" frontiers, the Pyrenees, the Alps and the Rhine, though there was to be no longer any French suzerainty or predominating influence beyond them. This offer, conveyed through St. Aignan, a French diplomat held as a prisoner of war, gave Napoleon what he so urgently needed, an opportunity of gaining time.

He probably had no intention, at this stage of the war, of accepting any such terms, though later there came a time when the allies' offers were much less favourable, and Napoleon claimed in vain the offer of the Frankfort terms. For the present, he delayed answering till the 1st December, and then made impossible proposals for the surrender of the fortresses on the Vistula and the Oder, on condition that their garrisons were sent back to him so that he could add them to his field army. He did promise to appoint Caulaincourt as his plenipotentiary to meet the agents of the allies, a promise which led to the assembling of the Congress of Châtillon in February 1814.

As regards the plan of campaign of the allies, there was never any chance of their adopting Blücher's energetic ideas. Various schemes, submitted by Knesebeck, Radetzky, and the Tsar himself, were discussed and rejected.

The scheme finally accepted laid down the following general movements:

(1) The main army (Army of Bohemia) to cross the Upper Rhine about Basle and even higher up, sending 12,000 men under Bubna to secure Switzerland, thereby giving the Austrians a more direct communication with their own country. The centre would move on the plateau of Langres, to which great importance was attached as turning by their sources the Meuse, the Marne, and the Seine; a truly 18th century view.

(2) Blücher with the Army of Silesia would, at the same time, cross the Middle Rhine between Mayence and Coblence. His function was to manoeuvre so as to hold the enemy until Schwarzenberg could reach his communications.

(3) Of the North Army the corps of Bülow and Winzingerode were to subdue Holland, whilst Bernadotte with the rest, reinforced by part of the Russian-Polish army of Bennigsen, dealt with Davout at Hamburg, and with the Danes.

The general principles of action of the divided armies were laid down in a memorandum of the 13th November by Schwarzenberg. It is understood to represent the scheme arrived at during the armistice of 1813. They were briefly:

(1) Fortresses encountered to be masked, not besieged.

(2) The main army to operate on the enemy's flank and communications.

(3) The enemy to be forced, by attacks on his communications, either to detach, or to hurry the bulk of his forces on the threatened points.

(4) He was only to be attacked when divided and very inferior in numbers.

(5) If the enemy advanced in mass against one of the allied armies, it would retire whilst the other advanced.

(6) The point of union of all allied forces to be the enemy's

15

headquarters.

The Bohemian army crossed the Rhine on the 20th December, 1813, Blücher on the 1st January, 1814, Winzingerode five days later.

Into the details of invasion we do not propose to enter until the end of January, when Napoleon again appears upon the scene. He had disposed his feeble forces in an immense "cordon" facing the Rhine. This very disposition clearly indicated that he had no intention of making a serious defence. All that this show of defence could do was to prevent the enemy occupying with light troops an area abandoned by the French. The allied advance to the Marne was therefore only a *promenade militaire*, though probably the marshals, in Napoleon's absence, might well have done more than they did to delay the enemy. They fell back as the allies advanced without any serious attempt at resistance, or even at delaying them by manoeuvring.

When he got back to Paris early in November, 1813, Napoleon was busy trying to raise a new army. Between the 9th October, 1813, and the 6th January, 1814, no less than 936,000 new levies of regular troops and National Guards were ordered, including drafts on all the years back to 1802, and forward to 1815. But, for various reasons, some of these levies were postponed; for some there were no arms available, and some were resisted or evaded. Houssaye calculates that not more than one-third were actually called up, and not more than one-eighth ever fought.

The Emperor might draw trained soldiers from the armies of Italy and of Spain, but he never could make up his mind, as his soldier's instinct bade him, to abandon the secondary objective in Italy. As for Spain, he endeavoured, too late, by restoring Ferdinand VII to his throne, to conclude a peace which should result in the withdrawal from the war of the English and Spanish armies, and the return to him of his veterans under Soult and Suchet.

The bottom was knocked out of his scheme by the refusal of the Spanish Cortés to ratify the treaty of Valençay, signed by Ferdinand whilst still a prisoner. Napoleon had to be satisfied with the withdrawal of part of Soult's and Suchet's veterans, [3] and their replacement by new levies. These-troops were, with the exception of the Old Guard, the best he had.

From Italy he withdrew nothing, and presently the Viceroy was opposed, not only by Bellegarde's Austrians, but also by the Neapolitan army when Murat abandoned his brother-in-law. In the Netherlands, Maison's 15,000 men were handicapped by a general uprising induced by Bülow's advance. The Emperor had nothing left but the resources of France. There, unpopular though he now was outside the army, he was able to do much in raising a general insurrection in the provinces occupied by the allies. They played into his hands here; for undoubtedly many atrocities (not perhaps worse than those of the French in Germany) were committed by the Cossacks and others. Though peasant risings caused much annoyance to the allies, and necessitated the strong guarding of convoys, it hardly seems that they had any serious influence on the result. They certainly added greatly to the savagery of the campaign on both sides. Into details of Napoleon's efforts to raise a new army we do not propose to enter at length. [4]

As for the allies, owing to the addition to their forces of those of the Rhenish Confederation, reinforcements were constantly coming in, and were sometimes sent to the front, sometimes employed in the task of blockading the fortresses, thus setting free the better trained troops at first so employed. Plotho calculates that the allies put into the field in 1814, one way or another, 652,000 men in first line and 235,000 in reserve; 887,000 in all. Of these 230,000 were Austrians; 278,000 Russians; 162,000 Prussians; 197,000 other Germans; and 20,000 Swedes. [5]

The "cordon" which the Emperor left facing the Rhine in November was generally disposed thus:

3. He withdrew altogether from Soult, to his own army, 11,015 infantry, 3420 cavalry and forty guns. From Suchet were taken, for Augereau's army of the Rhine, 8051 infantry, 2132 cavalry, and eighteen guns.
4. For a most graphic account of the difficulties in raising men and arms, and of the details of guerrilla warfare, see Houssaye, *1814*, Chap. 1.
5. The Austrians in Italy are included, but not the forces of Wellington.

Victor, with about 1 0,000 men, watched the Upper Rhine from Hünningen to Landau.

Marmont had about 13,000 between Landau and Coblence.

Sebastiani, with 4500, watched from Coblence to the Lippe.

Macdonald, on his left, had 11,500 for the space from the Lippe to Nimeguen.

On the extreme left were Maison's 15,000 in the Netherlands, on the extreme right were 1600 men at Lyons, the nucleus of a corps entrusted to Augereau.

Morand was blockaded with 15,000 in Mayence.

The only reserves behind the centre of this immense line were, at first, the Old Guard under Michel; two divisions of Young Guard forming under Ney at Metz, under the high-sounding title of the "Army of the Vosges"; and a few battalions under Mortier.

On the 12th January Napoleon dictated a long note [6] on the actual situation of France. With the usual optimism of these latter days, he proceeds to estimate that Schwarzenberg with 50,000 men, and Blücher with 30,000, were all that could arrive before Paris by the middle of February, when he would have 120,000 men in the field to oppose them, besides a garrison of 30,000 in the capital. At this time, he seems to have contemplated awaiting the arrival of the enemy before Paris.

He was determined "never to make any preparation for abandoning Paris, and to bury himself, if necessary, in its ruins." He had previously said that he intended to make of Paris a strong place which he would never quit. [7] He did not believe in the enemy's marching on Paris. He would certainly have been justified in the belief if his gross underestimate of the allied forces available had been nearly correct. Sometime during the next few days he was disillusioned, and resolved on a very different plan: an attempt to prevent the junction of Blücher and Schwarzenberg towards Châlons, and to defeat them separately.

6. *Corr.* 21,089.
7. *Corr.* 21,084 of 11th January.

The theatre of war with which we are mainly concerned is enclosed by a line running north-east from Paris to Laon, thence through Reims, Châlons-sur-Marne, St. Dizier, Chaumont, Châtillon-sur-Seine, Sens, and Fontainebleau back to Paris. It may be described generally as a plain except in the portion north of the river Aisne, where there are hills rising some 400 feet above the river levels. This area will be more fully described later on. The country between the Marne on the north and east and a line running roughly through Villenauxe, Sézanne, and Etoges is almost a dead level, scantily populated and with a heavy, clayey, marshy soil. The tract west of this line lies on a higher level and is much superior in fertility and population. It is also much more undulating with quite deep valleys in places.

The Seine and the Marne are the two principal rivers in the theatre. Always serious military obstacles, rarely fordable in winter even in their upper reaches, they flow more or less parallel to one another on the arc of a circle convex towards the southwest until they begin to converge to unite just outside Paris.

The Aube is the most important tributary joining the Seine on its right bank. It is generally unfordable within the theatre, except in very dry weather. The Seine receives a considerable tributary, the Yonne, on its left bank, and a smaller one, the Loing. The most important tributaries of the Marne from our point of view are the Grand and Petit Morin on the left bank, and the Ourcq on the right. The two former are petty streams, but their marshy beds give them some importance as military obstacles, a remark which applies with still greater force to the larger Ourcq.

The Aisne, flowing from east to west through Berry-au-Bac and Soissons, is a much more important stream, generally unfordable. Its tributary the Vesle, flowing through Reims and thence to its left bank above Soissons, is a small stream of secondary importance. The Lette, or Ailette, which flows parallel to and north of the Aisne, will be referred to later. Both it and the Aisne are tributaries of the Oise.

Three great roads led across the theatre to Paris.

(1) From Châlons-sur-Marne along the left bank of the Marne to Château-Thierry where it crossed to the right. At La Ferté-sous-Jouarre it recrossed to the left bank, and finally again went to the right bank at Trilport.

The chord of the arc made by this road between Châlons and La Ferté-sous-Jouarre was formed by an inferior road, though still a good one as roads then went, from Châlons by Champaubert and Montmirail direct to La Ferté, where it joined the *chaussée*.

(2) From Chaumont across the Aube at Bar-sur-Aube, then across the Seine at Troyes. At Nogent-sur-Seine it again crossed to the right bank of the Seine, finally crossing the Marne close to Paris.

(3) From Auxerre by the right bank of the Yonne to Sens, where it crossed to the left bank, passing again to the right bank of the Seine at Montereau, and joining (2) at the crossing of the Marne outside Paris.

There were many other roads of fair quality for the times, running both east and west, and north and south.

The *"chausses"* and other roads had to pass many times across the Seine, Marne, and other streams, and we shall find the bridges frequently destroyed and repaired, often in the course of a few days, by each side alternately. The facility or difficulty of restoration often exercised an important influence on the course of operations.

CHAPTER 2

Brienne and La Rothière

Napoleon, leaving Joseph in charge of Paris, of the Empress, and of the King of Rome, reached Châlons early on the 26th January, 1814. He had been preceded there by Lefebvre-Desnoettes at the head of 1700 Guard cavalry. The troops available for immediate operations were:

Victor with the 2nd corps and Milhaud with the 5th cavalry corps between Vitry and St. Dizier from which their advanced guard had been driven on the 25th.	14,747 [1]
Marmont with the 6th corps and Doumerc's 1st cavalry corps. He had only Lagrange's infantry at Vitry le Brulé and the cavalry. Ricard's division was on the march from St. Menehould to Vitry.	12,051
Ney with three divisions of Young Guard (Meunier's, Decouz's, and Rottembourg's) and Lefebvre-Desnoettes' cavalry at Châlons and Vitry.	14,505
Total	41,303

1. It must be remembered throughout this campaign that the terms "corps," "division," etc., on the French side do not necessarily represent anything like the numbers they did in former campaigns. A corps was sometimes a force only equal to one of the old brigades whilst a division sometimes only represented the strength of one or two battalions.

On the left, but out of reach for the present, were Macdonald and Sebastiani marching from Mézières to St. Menehould. After detaching garrisons, etc., they had not more than 10,000 or 11,000 men between them.

Mortier, who had about 20,000 men, of whom 12,000 were of the Guard, had fallen back on Troyes after an indecisive action with part of Schwarzenberg's army at Bar-sur-Aube. Of his force, Dufour's division of the Reserve of Paris was at Arcis-sur-Aube whither it had marched on the 25th by Lesmont, the bridge at which place Dufour had been unable to destroy as he passed. He was on the way to join Napoleon. Far away on the right was Allix with 2800 men towards Sens and Auxerre.

Napoleon had intended taking the offensive on the 26th, believing Victor to be at least as far forward as St. Dizier, and Dufour at Brienne. In the circumstances, he proposed to attack Blücher, whom he now believed to be at St. Dizier, on the 27th, before he could join Schwarzenberg's advanced corps. There was a trifling action at St. Dizier on the 27th, from which Napoleon learned that he was too late, and that Blücher was gone for Brienne, where he was due on the 28th.

The Prussian commander would there be in touch with Schwarzenberg's troops at Bar-sur-Aube, but there might still be time to drive him against the Aube at Brienne and inflict a severe blow on him before he could be strongly supported. Napoleon also knew that he had broken in between Blücher and Yorck, who had been at Pont-à-Mousson on the morning of the 26th, where he received an order to rejoin Blücher at once. [2]

Mortier had been ordered to join Napoleon by Dienville and Brienne, but, on the 27th, the Emperor, hearing of his retreat on Troyes, ordered him to Arcis, provided that movement would not endanger Troyes. Despatches to the same effect sent by Berthier to Mortier, to Bordessoulle,[3] and to Colbert at Nogent, were intercepted by Cossacks, and from them Blücher as-

---

2.Yorck had been relieved in the blockade of Metz by a force, under Borosdin, detached by Langeron from before Mayence.

3.At Arcis with 1000 cavalry.

certained, though only on the morning of the 29th, that he had Napoleon descending on his rear with 30,000 or 40,000 men, between himself and Yorck. So late as the morning of the 28th, Blücher had written of the affair at St. Dizier that the enemy with only badly organized troops could do nothing against the allied lines of communication, and, "if he tries it, nevertheless, nothing more desirable can happen for us; then we shall get Paris without a blow."[4]

The Emperor ordered the advance on Brienne in three columns.

Right—Gérard with Dufour's and Ricard's [5] divisions, and Piquet's cavalry direct on Brienne from Vitry;

Centre—the Guard by Eclaron on Montier-en-Der;

Left—Victor and Milhaud up the left bank of the Marne to Rochecourt, whence they would turn through Vassy to Montier-en-Der. Marmont was left behind with Lagrange's division and the 1st cavalry corps, having a rear-guard at Bar-le-Duc, to keep back Yorck.

The roads were in a fearful condition owing to the thaw which had set in. Nevertheless, Napoleon's troops managed to get over them, so that by evening on the 28th Gérard was with Dufour's division at Braux-le-Comte, Ricard's behind, and Piquet's cavalry making for Montier-en-Der, which it reached early on the 29th.

The centre and left were with Napoleon at Montier-en-Der and Vassy. During this day Marmont's rearguard evacuated Bar-le-Duc, which was occupied by Yorck.

Marmont, leaving 800 infantry and 400 cavalry at St Dizier under Lagrange, to protect his rear against Yorck, marched off with the rest for Eclaron.

Of the enemy Blücher, reaching Brienne, had kept Olsufiew's corps there and had sent Sacken's across the Lesmont bridge, by the left bank of the Aube on the road to Arcis-sur-Aube. In that

4. Janson, 1. 155.
5. Of Marmont's (6th) corps.

position Sacken received orders from Blücher, who had now heard of the fight at St. Dizier on the 27th, directing him to concentrate on Pougy and Lesmont. His cavalry was at Ramerupt and Piney.

Wittgenstein with the 6th corps of the Bohemian army, was at Haudelincourt on the Ornain, on his march from Toul to Joinville. His advanced guard, under Pahlen, had, however, got so far forward as to be with Blücher at Brienne. Lanskoi, retreating from St. Dizier on the 27th, had got to Doulevant and Dommartin.

Schwarzenberg's headquarters were at Chaumont; Wrede with the 5th corps was about ten miles out on the road from Chaumont to St. Dizier; the Crown Prince of Würtemberg (4th corps) was at Bar-sur-Aube; Gyulai with the 3rd corps between Bar and Vendœuvre; Colloredo (1st corps) was on the march from Châtillon towards Sens, and Platow's Cossacks at Auxon.[6] Barclay with the Reserves was on the road from Langres to Chaumont.

On the 29th Napoleon's advance continued in two columns. At this time he was under two misapprehensions;

(1) he believed Dufour had destroyed the Lesmont bridge, and
(2) being ignorant of the interception of Berthier's despatch to Mortier, he believed that the orders would result in the arrival of Mortier, Bordessoulle, and Colbert.

He was feeling his way, and, until further enlightened by reconnaissance, did not feel in a position to prescribe further. For the present Blücher had only the weak corps of Olsufiew [7] (about 6000 men) and Pahlen's advanced guard of Wittgenstein's corps (about 3000 sabres).

Olsufiew was posted by Blücher in Brienne, whilst Pahlen's cavalry was to deploy on the plain to the north-east. Lanskoi,

---

6. It will be noticed that the 2nd corps is omitted. It had been left behind to support Bubna's operations in Switzerland.
7. Olsufiew commanded two Russian infantry divisions (Udom and Karnilev) belonging to Langeron's corps.

with part of Sacken's cavalry (about 1600), was opposite the southern end of the Bois d'Ajou.

When Grouchy debouched from that wood he found himself opposed to all this cavalry, and it was not till between 2 and 3 p.m. that he felt himself sufficiently strong to attack. Pahlen then slowly retired through Brienne to take post south of it, on the road to Bar-sur-Aube.

Grouchy's attack on his rearmost regiments was at first successful, but in the end was beaten off with the loss of three guns.

Sacken's infantry had now partly come up, and were posted across the road from Brienne to Bar-sur-Aube, Olsufiew remaining in Brienne.

Such was the position when Napoleon, arriving on the battlefield, ordered a heavy artillery fire on Brienne and Sacken's troops, under cover of which Victor deployed with Duhesme's division debouching from the wood of Ajou. At first, Duhesme succeeded in getting into part of Brienne, but was driven out again, losing two guns which he had taken from the enemy. The Emperor now ordered a general attack by the infantry. It was between 5 and 6 p.m., almost dark, when Ney, delayed by the badness of the roads, was ready to join in this attack. He advanced with six of Decouz's battalions against Brienne by the Maizières road, whilst Duhesme on his left renewed his attack from the Bois d'Ajou.

On the other side, most of Sacken's corps had passed through Brienne, though his trains were still partly on the road there from Lesmont, where the bridge had been destroyed after their passage. Pahlen's cavalry was on the allied right, whilst the French cavalry was all on the opposite wing, north-east of Brienne.

As the French infantry advanced on Brienne, Duhesme's division was charged in left flank by the whole of Pahlen's and Lanskoi's cavalry, to which Napoleon could oppose none of the same arm.

Duhesme's men were driven in confusion on Decouz's with the loss of eight guns, and only the gathering darkness saved a complete disaster.

Blücher and Gneisenau, believing the fighting to be over for the day, retired to the *château* where they narrowly escaped capture by Victor's leading brigade under General Chataux, which surprised the chateau by an unguarded road. Chataux then descended on the town and drove Olsufiew's men almost completely from it. Again Blücher and Gneisenau, as well as Sacken, narrowly escaped capture. Lefebvre-Desnoette's cavalry had also broken into Brienne by the Lesmont road. As Sacken's trains were still not past Brienne and in great danger of capture, Blücher ordered Sacken to retake the town, whilst Olsufiew stormed the *château*.

Olsufiew completely failed, but Sacken, after a desperate house-to-house struggle, had, by midnight, driven the French almost completely from Brienne, though they still held the chateau. Then, at last, the fighting ceased. The day had cost each side about 3000 men. On the French side Admiral Baste was killed, and Decouz mortally wounded. Napoleon, with headquarters at Perthes, posted his infantry on either side of the Maizières road.

Blücher now ordered a silent retreat from Brienne on Bassancourt, covered by the cavalry. This was unmolested by the French who only re-entered Brienne at 4 a.m.

The battle of Brienne was scarcely a tactical victory for Napoleon; strategically it was little short of a defeat, for he had failed in his attempt to destroy Blücher before he could be supported by Schwarzenberg. Blücher honestly admitted having taken the attack on St. Dizier for a mere demonstration.[8] He only fully realized the position when he read Berthier's captured despatch on the morning of the 29th. Perhaps his best course then would have been to order Sacken up the left bank of the Aube, to destroy the bridge at Lesmont, and to make for that at Dienville or higher up. Meanwhile, Blücher, amusing the enemy with a rearguard action, could have retreated on Bar-sur-Aube towards Schwarzenberg.

---

8. Weil, 1. 420.

That, however, would have been a course repugnant to the bold spirit of the old Prussian. Perhaps, too, he might apprehend danger to Sacken from an attack by Mortier before he could pass to the right bank of the Aube at Dienville or higher up. Napoleon certainly made a grave tactical mistake in keeping all his cavalry on the right, whilst Blücher's was all on the opposite wing. There was thus no cavalry to protect Duhesme's left as he advanced on Brienne. The French attack was completely driven back by the success of the allied cavalry which Blücher used with great wisdom and just at the psychological moment.

Both Napoleon and Blücher were compelled to bring their troops into action piecemeal; the former because, if he was to gain the tactical result he hoped for, he was bound to begin early, before Blücher could slip away; Blücher, owing to the absence of Sacken at the beginning of the action.

Napoleon was unfortunate in just missing the capture of Blücher and Gneisenau, who only left one side of the courtyard of the *château* as French troops entered by the other. It is almost impossible to estimate the influence on the whole course of the campaign which would have been exercised by the capture of these two generals, representing as they did almost the whole of the energy and determination on the side of the allies.

Whilst Napoleon was following Blücher to Brienne, Yorck, now completely cut from his chief, had occupied Bar-le-Duc on the 28th, when it was evacuated by Marmont's rearguard. Arriving before St. Dizier next day, he found himself in communication with Wittgenstein at Joinville. The latter, as well as Wrede, had been ordered towards Joinville, in order to meet the then expected attack on the allied communications. Both were there on the 29th, and found that Marmont was holding Vassy and Doulevant strongly. Wrede's men were too exhausted by their march to undertake anything on the 30th.

When the Crown Prince of Würtemberg, on the 28th, pushed his outposts down the right bank of the Aube, he was surprised to find Blücher in front of him in that direction. He met Blücher personally, and it was arranged between them that the Würtemberg corps (4th) should remain in support of Blücher so long as he was on this part of the Aube.

Schwarzenberg was equally surprised to find Blücher where he was, and highly disapproved his having abandoned the great road through Châlons to Nancy from which he feared Napoleon might operate against his communications. He had no idea of following the bold plan of a decisive advance on Paris, which Blücher still advocated. He accordingly ordered the 4th corps and the 3rd (Gyulai) merely to be prepared to rescue and support Blücher if he should be in difficulties. Gyulai at this time was at Vendœuvre, with advanced guards watching Mortier towards Troyes. At the same time, the Russo-Prussian reserves were slowly following the 3rd and 4th Corps from Langres, and Colloredo, with the 1st Corps, was under orders to hold Bar-sur-Seine against a French movement from Troyes on Dijon, aiming at Schwarzenberg's communications in that direction. The commander-in-chief was much alarmed at the prospect of such a movement which, however, he seems to have had no sufficient reason to expect.

There had been trouble with Platow, who was unaccountably inert and was only induced on the 27th to get off the line of the advance on Troyes and to move on Sens, whence, on the 29th, he failed to drive 500 or 600 French. The allies held one of their numerous councils of war at Chaumont on the 29th January, and at it it was decided to inform Caulaincourt, Napoleon's plenipotentiary, that the congress for the discussion of terms of peace was proposed for assembly at Châtillon on the 3rd February. On the military side it was decided

(1) The 3rd and 4th corps to concentrate at Bar-sur-Aube.
(2) The right wing (5th and 6th corps) at Joinville, ready to attack Vassy on the 31st January.
(3) Colloredo with the left (I corps) to move from Bar-sur-Seine on Vendœuvre, where he would replace Gyulai by the 31st at latest.
Thence he would threaten the French right and rear and

be in a position to stop any attempt by Mortier to advance from Troyes.

(4) Yorck and Kleist to be ordered to hurry forward towards the army of Bohemia.

On the morning of the 30th Blücher had retired on the neighbourhood of Trannes and Eclance, where he appeared to intend holding fast. On that day Yorck occupied St. Dizier, now evacuated by Lagrange, whose march to Montier-en-Der was somewhat harassed by Yorck s cavalry, and who might have been seriously compromised had Wittgenstein co-operated from Joinville with the Prussians. There was little or no co-operation between the allied commanders, and it was only a matter of chance when they knew anything about one another's movements.

Blücher's position at Trannes was unaltered on the 31st January. The 4th corps was on his right rear between Maisons and Fresnay; Gyulai was about Bassancourt, with outposts towards Vendœuvre. The reserves were echeloned from Bar-sur-Aube to some distance towards Chaumont. Wrede, with his infantry at Doulevant and on the road to Soulaines, had cavalry nearly up to Sommevoire and at Soulaines. Wittgenstein was at Montier-en-Der, with cavalry as far forward as Chavanges. Yorck was approaching Vitry from St. Dizier.

Napoleon's movements on the 30th and 31st were not many. Mortier moved a large part of his force from Troyes to Arcis-sur-Aube, but brought it back on the 31st. Macdonald was at Châlons. Marmont moved from Vassy on Montier-en-Der. Thence, instead of making direct for Brienne, he made for Soulaines, apparently with a view to using a better, though longer road. Meanwhile, at 1 p.m. on the 31st, the Emperor had sent him orders to march for Lesmont (leaving a rearguard at Maizières), to complete the restoration of the bridge, and to send an advanced guard across the Aube to Piney.

As, however, Marmont received these orders at Soulaines, he naturally could not execute them, and the Emperor appears to have expected that, having reached Soulaines, he would hold it. In the evening, however, the Duke of Ragusa was alarmed by the appearance of Pahlen, who was carrying out his orders to rejoin Wittgenstein. Though he showed no signs of any intention to attack, Marmont thought it necessary to fall back to Morvilliers where he arrived, after a fatiguing night march, at 1 a.m. on the 1st February. The consequence of this move was that the direct road to Brienne through the Soulaines forest was left open to Wrede. Wittgenstein's cavalry surprised and cut up the rearguard left by Marmont at Montier-en-Der, driving the remains back on Pougy and Lesmont.

On the 31st January the allies decided to attack Napoleon next day. The immediate command in the battle was delegated to Blücher, perhaps largely with the idea of placating him. But he was not given full command of all the forces including his reserves. All that were under his absolute command were his own two corps (Sacken and Olsufiew), the 3rd (Gyulai) and the 4th (Würtemberg). Two divisions of Russian *cuirassiers* and two of grenadiers were to replace him at Trannes as he advanced; one division of Russian Guards was to take post at Ailleville, one at Fresnay. None of these reserves were made over to Blücher.

The positions of both Wittgenstein and Wrede marked them out for use against Napoleon's left and rear; but Wittgenstein was ordered to march away from the battlefield by following Yorck to St. Dizier. Wrede was to follow Wittgenstein by Montier-en-Der. There was really no reason why Yorck, as well as these two, should not have been brought down on Napoleon's communications with Lesmont. He could have contained Macdonald's weak corps with a rearguard. Fortunately, a letter from Wrede crossed the orders sent to him. He said that, as Wittgenstein, at Vassy, was practically unopposed, he proposed himself to move westwards on Brienne, and suggested the use of Wittgenstein also.

Schwarzenberg at once ignored his own orders and replied that Wrede's proposed movement was precisely what he desired. He did not, however, modify the orders to Wittgenstein. Blücher was to be allowed to "try a battle," but, as Weil concludes, the order that the 3rd and 4th corps were not to go beyond Brienne, and the omission to give Blücher control of his reserves, and of Wrede's corps, plainly show that he was not intended to be allowed to reap the full fruits of victory. A decisive victory was not what was desired by the Austrian politicians.

Barclay de Tolly, commanding the Guards and Reserves, took upon himself to modify Schwarzenberg's orders by keeping both divisions of the Russian Guard at Ailleville, as well as the whole Prussian Guard. They were to move up to Trannes by 4 p.m. on the 1st February.

Wrede had suggested to Blücher some delay in the frontal attack, in order to give him time to approach Napoleon's left flank from Soulaines.

Blüchers command comprised, in round numbers:

(1) The two corps of the Silesian army	27,000
(2) The 3rd corps (Gyulai), less one division left to await relief by Colloredo at Vendœuvre	12,000
(3) 4th corps (Würtemberg)	14,000
	53,000

Wrede was co-operating with another 26,000, and behind Blücher were 34,000 Guards and Reserves of Barclay, of whom only 6000 or 7000 actually came into action. Altogether the allies engaged some 85,000 men and about 200 guns to whom Napoleon could only hope to oppose:

(1) Gérard	8,300
(2) Victor	17,300
(3) Marmont	8,200
(4) Ney	11,300
	45,100 with 128 guns.

If the allies had utilized the whole of the Guards and Reserves, as well as Wittgenstein, they would have had nearly three times the French strength.

It is almost inconceivable that Napoleon, knowing his inferiority, especially in cavalry, should have deliberately chosen the southern and eastern edges of the plain of Brienne as a position for a defensive battle. As a matter of fact, the dead level open plain was not quite so favourable for a superior cavalry as it usually was; for a frost in the night had given a slippery coating to the slush of the recent thaw, and the plain was covered with snow which had been falling during the night, and continued to do so, with brief intervals, during the 1st February.

Napoleon has been much blamed by Clausewitz for fighting as he did, but the Prussian critic had not, when he wrote, seen Napoleon's orders, which show clearly that he did not intend fighting at all. His first orders, passed after an early reconnaissance, aimed at a retreat to Troyes by Lesmont, which was actually commenced by the despatch of Ney through Brienne to Lesmont. The Emperor was in complete uncertainty as to Blüchers movements, and thought it quite probable that the allies meant to detain him towards Brienne whilst they moved with their main force by Vendœuvre against Mortier's weak force at Troyes. It was this idea which induced him to decide on retreat.

About noon, in consequence of reports from Victor and Grouchy, he again went out to reconnoitre, and was soon convinced that a general attack of the allies was about to fall upon him, that it was too late to retreat, and that he must fight a battle even in his disadvantageous position. Ney's retreat was immediately stopped. He was already between Brienne and Lesmont with two divisions; only Rottembourg's was as far back as Brienne-la-Vieille, and it must be some hours before the other two could be back.

Napoleon, with his weak force, could do little more than hold the villages on his extended front with infantry, and fill the intervening spaces with cavalry.

On his right, Dienville, a fair-sized village with a bridge over the Aube, was held by Gérard's 8000 men who extended part of the way to the next village, La Rothière. Eight squadrons of cavalry (Piquet) united the left of Gérard to the right of Duhesme (Victor's corps) who had one brigade in the small and not very defensible village of La Rothière, on the Brienne-Trannes road a mile east of Dienville, and one behind it. Two battalions were in each of the villages of Petit Mesnil and Chaumesnil, and Victor had, of his second division, one battalion in the wood of Beaulieu, four battalions on the heights behind it, and the rest in the hamlet of La Giberie. All these were in the very low hills just outside the plain. Grouchy, with Pirè's and l'Héritier's cavalry, was on the plain between Petit Mesnil and Chaumesnil; Nansouty, with the Guard cavalry divisions of Lefebvre-Desnoettes, Colbert, and Guyot, on Grouchy's right, between Petit Mesnil and La Rothière.

On the extreme left was Marmont about Morvilliers with Lagrange's division, with a battalion in La Chaise on the Soulaines road, and Doumerc's cavalry behind it. Leaving out of account for the present Ney's reserve of 11,300, of which Rottembourg alone was as near as Brienne-la-Vieille, Napoleon had less than 34,000 men spread along a line of some seven miles from Dienville to beyond Morvilliers. The space was far too great for his strength.

It was about noon when Sacken's corps began to advance from Trannes against La Rothière, with Olsufiew following. The roads were so bad that he had to leave half of his 72 guns in order to give double teams to the rest. When these, in front of the infantry, were within musket shot of La Rothière, they were left deployed whilst the teams went back for the rest. Even their cavalry escort was not yet up when Nansouty's cavalry bore down on them. It was only thanks to the admirable service of the Russian guns that Nansouty was stopped by a storm of grape.

Just as Sacken's infantry began to deploy there was a temporary cessation of the snow which exposed them to the full view and fire of the French.

Again Nansouty charged, carried away Lanskoi's cavalry, and was just descending on the infantry when he was attacked in front and flank by four fresh cavalry regiments and completely defeated, with the loss of twenty-four guns. Had Sacken at once advanced, he would probably have carried La Rothière, broken the French centre, and hemmed their right against the Aube. But Blücher had not seen this cavalry affair on account of the snow, and when he heard of it the opportunity was lost. It was 4 p.m. when Sacken was ready to attack La Rothière. About the same hour Gyulai, who had been directed on Dienville, arrived on the battlefield. He had sent a whole division across the Aube at Unienville as he passed, with orders to attack Dienville from the left bank, and he had on the right bank only Grummer's brigade and Spleny's [9]

On Sacken's right the 4th corps had cleared the Beaulieu wood and advanced with some difficulty on La Giberie, which was taken but lost again to a counter attack by Victor. The Crown Prince, thinking his position critical, urged Wrede to attack Chaumesnil, and demanded reinforcements from Toll, who happened to be with him. Toll, without informing Blücher, appears to have ordered both the divisions of Russian *cuirassiers* and one of grenadiers from Trannes.[10]

Wrede had been slow in his march, partly because Pahlen, on his way to rejoin Wittgenstein, crossed his line, and partly on account of difficult roads. He appeared in front of La Chaise about 2 p.m. Marmont, endeavouring to concentrate to his right, was also hampered by bad roads. Shortly before 4 p.m. Wrede's vastly superior forces had driven Victor's infantry on the Bois d'Ajou, where they were covered by Doumerc's cavalry. He had lost at least one battery surprised by Cossacks.

When Wrede received the Crown Prince's call for help towards Chaumesnil, he attacked that place and captured it without much difficulty. The loss of this village greatly alarmed Napoleon who himself led towards it Guyot's cavalry and Meunier's Young Guard division. Attack after attack was launched but failed to make any impression on Wrede's strong position. By 7 p.m. the French guns in this quarter were silenced, and Wrede's cavalry,

---

9. There were two generals of this name engaged in the battle who must not be confused: (a) Major-General von Spleny commanding a brigade of the 3rd corps; (b) Lieutenant Feldmarschall von Spleny commanding an Austrian division of Wrede's corps on the extreme right.
10. It will be remembered that they were excluded from Blücher's command.

penetrating between the infantry squares, captured twenty-one pieces. It was pitch dark when Marmont and Meunier fell back towards Brienne. Marmont's left brigade at Morvilliers had been driven by Spleny behind the Bois d'Ajou. Wrede's successes greatly lightened the Würtembergers' task. By 5 p.m. they had again taken La Giberie after a fierce struggle, which was repeated later at Petit Mesnil. When the two leading brigades took Petit Mesnil the main body had still only got as far as La Giberie, so difficult was the road to it.

Blücher had fixed his eyes on the capture of La Rothière as the centre of Napoleon's line. About 4 p.m. Sacken's 16,000 men advanced with the bayonet; for, as so often happened in those days of flint locks, the primings had been damped by the snow and the muskets would not go off. Duhesme, with only some 4000 men, was driven out towards Petit Mesnil, though the French fought desperately.

Even then a handful of veterans barricaded themselves in the northern houses and held them against all Sacken's efforts. Nor could Sacken's men debouch from La Rothière. As they tried to do so they were charged by Colbert's cavalry and forced to fall back on Olsufiew's corps behind them. Blücher now sent for the *cuirassiers* and grenadiers from Trannes. But both divisions of *cuirassiers* and one of grenadiers had been taken by Toll to help the 4th Corps, and they marched and counter-marched without ever doing any fighting. The other grenadier division at last reached La Rothière. Blücher had also called up Grummer's brigade, from in front of Dienville, to aid at La Rothière.

Thus Gyulai, when ordered at 5 p.m. to attack Dienville, could only do so with artillery on the right bank; for he had no infantry but Spleny's four battalions. His division on the left bank did, indeed, for a moment, get possession of the bridge but was promptly driven back. It was only at midnight, when the French had evacuated it, that Gyulai occupied Dienville.

Napoleon, witnessing the advance of Wrede, saw that the battle was lost, and that he could do no more than cover the retreat on Lesmont. Ordering Grouchy to use his cavalry to support

Victor against the 4th Corps, and Nansouty to hold firm behind La Rothière, he sent Oudinot with Rottembourg's division to retake that village. As night fell the leading brigade retook La Rothière in face of a terrible fire, but then, meeting Olsufiew's men, was again driven out. Oudinot with the 2nd Brigade once more stormed the village, beyond which they met the Russian grenadiers from Trannes and Grummer's brigade from Gyulai's corps.

By these fresh troops Rottembourg's exhausted men were finally driven out, though they reformed 500 paces north of La Rothière. It was 8 p.m., pitch dark except where the scene was lighted by the burning village. The cavalry of Wrede and Würtemberg had just had to desist from a final charge on Victor and Marmont, because they found themselves charging one another in the darkness. Napoleon now set Drouot with all available guns to check the enemy's advance from La Rothière. By 9 p.m., when it was snowing harder than ever, the pursuit ceased.

In this sanguinary battle Napoleon lost some 6000 men, including 2000 prisoners, and fifty or sixty guns. The allies lost about the same number of men. The brunt was borne by Sacken who lost about 4000.

The allies had undoubtedly gained a notable victory over the man whom even Leipzig had not altogether robbed of his reputation for invincibility, and they were proportionately elated. The victory might well have been decisive of the whole campaign but for the orders which crippled Blücher, by leaving him without full control of the numerous reserves which might have been brought up from Trannes and Ailleville, and moreover sent Wittgenstein directly away from the battlefield, instead of bringing him down on Napoleon's rear. As we have said, a really decisive victory was not part of the Austrian programme at any rate. With the orders for the 3rd and 4th Corps not to proceed beyond Brienne in case of success, there was clearly little chance of Blücher's being able to make his success as complete as it might have been.

As for the conduct of the battle, Blücher confined his attention mainly to his centre and left at La Rothière and Dienville. Against the former he sent 22,000 men, followed eventually by one Russian grenadier division and Grummer's brigade. Had he had the other grenadier division, and still better the two divisions of *cuirassiers*, he might have been able to drive Napoleon's centre back on Brienne and cut off Gérard in Dienville. But these troops had been ordered, without his knowledge, to support Würtemberg, who did not really want them, as he was relieved by Wrede's attack on Chaumesnil.

In the end, these three divisions wandered about and did nothing. For this Blücher was in no way responsible. But he made a mistake in pressing the attack on La Rothière with such obstinacy. Once Wrede was on the field, the French left was the place on which to concentrate the greatest efforts. Gyulai's despatch of a division to the left bank of the Aube appears to have been his own idea. When he was still further weakened on the right bank by having to detach Grummer, he had nothing left with which to attack Dienville in front. There was little chance of success for the attack from the left bank by the single bridge, which might quite possibly have been destroyed by Gérard; for, under the circumstances, Napoleon was not in the least likely to want it for retreat.

Much, if not most, of the credit for the victory is due to Wrede's successful resistance of Schwarzenberg's order to him to follow Wittgenstein. Had Schwarzenberg accepted Wrede's proposal to use Wittgenstein also against Napoleon's communications with Lesmont, the Emperor would probably have been compelled to retreat over the single bridge between Brienne and Radonvilliers. On the French side, as we have already shown, Napoleon probably intended to retreat on Lesmont, but found himself too late to avoid a battle.

His inaction about Brienne on the 30th and 31st January, when he did nothing beyond some cavalry reconnaissances, requires explanation. As has been argued by Commandant Weil, he probably wished to avoid retreat till the last moment on account of the effects which such a retreat might have on opinion in Paris. At Brienne he was in a central position, whence he could move in any direction according to circumstances. He had already passed orders sending Gérard to reinforce Mortier at Troyes, and calculated that that marshal would then have 27,000 men.[11] He had also approved Berthier's proposal to send army headquarters to Arcis-sur-Aube.[12] All this points to an intention to retire from Brienne. Where the Emperor failed was in holding on just too long.

The French fought splendidly at La Rothière, especially Rottembourg's 5000 men in the evening. Nansouty's attack on the Russian guns before the village earlier in the day should have been a great success but for the admirable service of the gunners. The Russian artillery was the best the allies had, and it was a point of honour with them not to lose a gun. Nansouty was again unfortunate in his attack on Lanskoi's cavalry.

Of allied corps not on the field of battle, Wittgenstein reached St. Dizier. Yorck was in front of Vitry, which was not open to a *coup de main*. He there learnt that Macdonald was at Châlons, about to march on Vitry. Colloredo only reached Vendœuvre in the afternoon, where he relieved the light division left by Gyulai. He did not come into serious collision with Mortier who was still about Troyes.

Platow, on the 1st February, failed in an attack on Allix at Sens. Kleist was still only between Thionville and Metz; Kapzewitch was within a day's march of Nancy. Both were on the way to join Yorck.

---

11. That is 15,000 of his own, 8000 of Gérard and 4000 of the 2nd division Reserve of Paris under Hamelinaye. *Corr.* 21,162.
12. *Corr.* 21,159.

CHAPTER 3

The Retreat after La Rothière

Napoleon spent the night of the 1st to 2nd February in the Château of Brienne so familiar to him as a student, now seen by him for the last time. It was only at 11 p.m. that he was sure the enemy was not continuing the pursuit with fresh troops. He then decided on retreat by Lesmont on Troyes. Ricard was to cross the Aube by the bridge west of Brienne-la-Vieille, moving on Piney to cover the Lesmont-Troyes road. Gérard would act as rearguard at Brienne-la-Vieille, supported by Nansouty's cavalry. Curial's and Meunier's divisions were to wait for Gérard at Brienne-le Château, Rottembourg to take post on the heights half-way to Lesmont, becoming in his turn rear- guard as the others passed. Marmont to start at 3 a.m. and take post at Perthes en Rothière, whence he would retire later behind the Voire, and, if pressed, retreat again on Arcis by the right bank of the Aube. Macdonald, to whom the full extent of the defeat was not disclosed, was to manoeuvre to keep open the country between the Aube and the Marne. The Emperor was already meditating a fresh offensive from Arcis, as soon as he should receive the 12,000 or 14,000 troops recalled from Soult's army in the south.

The allies only started at 8 a.m. on the 2nd February, so that there were only a few small fights with the Emperor's rearguard up to Lesmont, where he got safely across the Aube and destroyed the bridge effectually.

Wrede followed Marmont who retired to the heights of Rosnay on the right bank of the Voire. There he fought a rearguard action, and eventually concealed his retreat on Arcis with such ability that Wrede completely lost touch of him.

An attempt to intercept the Arcis-Troyes road by Piney with the Russian cavalry and grenadiers was beaten off by Grouchy and Ricard. There was a good deal of confusion in Vendœuvre, owing to the unintended meeting there of Colloredo and the Guards and Reserves.

Wittgenstein, about to march on Vitry, found himself ordered back to Montier-en-Der. Yorck, about to attack Vitry, had to be satisfied with masking it, as his advanced guard was in contact with Macdonald on the Châlons road, and the marshal had to be met. Blücher, meanwhile, had had to stop at Brienne for a council of war held at the chateau at 9 a.m. At it were present the Tsar, the King of Prussia, Schwarzenberg, Blücher, and Barclay. Their views still varied as widely as ever as to the conduct of the campaign. At this moment they held the decision in their hands; for, with their great superiority of numbers, with Napoleon heavily defeated, there could be no doubt that, even after the time that had been lost, a direct and deter- mined advance on Paris must have succeeded.

There was no need to think of Macdonald's small force, which could have been easily contained by Yorck alone, and defeated when Kleist and Kapzewitch reached him. But, as before, a summary settlement of the war was not in the Austrian programme. Schwarzenberg advocated separation of the armies again, on the ground of difficulty of supply of so large a force on a single line. Blücher was not unwilling to follow this course which would give him some freedom of action, and prevent his being held back by Schwarzenberg's intolerable slowness. Clausewitz thinks that the separation was partly due to the exaggerated importance attributed to the victory of La Rothière, and the belief that either of the allied armies was alone capable of dealing with Napoleon. Anyhow, whatever the motives, the decisions arrived at were—

(1) The armies to separate.

(2) Blücher to march on Châlons, to rally to himself Yorck, Kleist, Kapzewitch, and Langeron, and then to march by the left bank of the Marne to Meaux.

(3) The army of Bohemia to advance on Troyes, and thence, by both banks of the Seine, on Paris.

(4) Wittgenstein and Seslawin's Cossacks were to form a connecting link between the armies.

Napoleon, meanwhile, had already divined the probable movements of the enemy. He wrote from Piney to Clarke on the 2nd February: "I shall be at Troyes tomorrow. It is possible that the army of Blücher may move to between the Aube and the Marne, towards Vitry and Châlons. From Troyes I shall operate, according to circumstances, to retard the movement of the column which I am assured is marching by Sens on Paris, or else to return and manoeuvre against Blücher to delay his march." [1]

On the evening of the 2nd the allies had so completely lost touch of the Emperor that they could not make up their minds which to believe of two cavalry reports, one saying the main body was retreating on Troyes, the other that it was on the road to Vitry.

On the 3rd February the allies did practically nothing, except Blücher who made progress in his march to the Marne. The 3rd, 4th, and 5th corps were unable to repair the bridge at Lesmont which the French had burnt to the water's edge. It was only in the evening that it struck anybody to march them up the right bank and cross at Dienville where the bridge was intact. [2]

Napoleon on this day (3rd) safely reached Troyes with all his army except Marmont, left for the present at Arcis. As soon as Schwarzenberg realized that Napoleon was retreating on Troyes, he began to believe the Emperor was moving on Bar-sur-Seine

1. *Corr.* 21,169. This letter disposes of Marmont's claim to be the real author of the idea of the attack on Blücher.
2. It seems a mistake that Gérard had not destroyed it. Ricard was ordered to destroy the bridge below after he had crossed. Probably the solidity of the Dienville bridge saved it, as it would be difficult for Gérard to blow it up in presence of the enemy.

to outflank his left and threaten his communications with Dijon.

This made him desire to shift the centre of gravity of his army leftwards, and to draw Wittgenstein, the connecting link with Blücher, to the left bank of the Aube. On the 4th, again, the allies made little progress. Colloredo was on both banks of the Seine, but did not venture to attack the French on the Barse where some offensive movements by Napoleon greatly alarmed Schwarzenberg. The 3rd and 4th corps were only just over the Dienville bridge, Wrede still between Brienne and Dienville. Wittgenstein was at Montier-en-Der with cavalry moving towards Plancy.

On the French side, the most important movement was Marmont's rather feeble retreat from Arcis on Méry, after burning all the bridges on the Aube near Arcis. As Berthier told him, this cut him from Macdonald, endangered convoys on the way from Paris, and, finally, prevented the Emperor from moving by Arcis against Blücher, should he desire to do so.

On this day (4th) Schwarzenberg wrote to Blücher explaining that he was moving leftwards, in accordance with the general principles of his own memorandum of the 13th November, in order to outflank Napoleon's right, or at least to cut off the troops known to be coming from Soult's army. He gives away the real motive of his move when he adds that it will reassure him as to his own left, and give him free use of an excellent line of retreat on Dijon.[3] He says nothing about Seslawin, who was watching Marmont and acting as a link with Blücher, a role which he would presumably continue to follow.

By the evening of the 5th February the Russo-Prussian Guards, followed by Colloredo, had reached Bar-sur-Seine. The 3rd and 4th corps had relieved Colloredo in front of the Barse, with the 5th (Wrede) behind them, and Wittgenstein at Piney, with Pahlen at Charmont. Any forward movement towards Troyes had been checked by the failure of an attack on the La Guillotière bridge, and by a threatened advance of Mortier at

3. Weil, 2. 17.

Maisons Blanches on the left bank of the Seine.

Seslawin was now ordered [4] from the extreme right to the extreme left, and Blücher was not informed of the movement. As he had no staff officer of his own with Seslawin, and that commander sent no information of his movement, Blücher was quite unaware of the fact that his connecting link with the army of Bohemia was gone, and that there was nothing to watch the enemy's movements in the space between the two armies. The serious consequences following on this will appear later.

During the 5th, Napoleon was preparing to retreat on Nogent-sur-Seine, a move on which he finally decided on hearing that Macdonald had abandoned Châlons before the advance of Yorck. He now decided to march against the left flank of Blüchers army, leaving a force to contain Schwarzenberg. The retreat was begun on the 6th, masked by leaving Mortier and Gérard at Troyes, with a few cavalry on the Barse and at Maisons Blanches, and Ricard at Méry. They were still in these positions on the evening of the 6th. Marmont was at Nogent; Napoleon with the rest halfway between Troyes and Nogent. On the extreme right were Pajol and Allix, on the Yonne at Montereau and Sens.

It was not till the afternoon of the 7th that Schwarzenberg, about to make a general attack on Troyes, discovered that it had been evacuated, Mortier and Gérard having now followed the Emperor to the western side of the great northward bend of the Seine. Though his army had certainly not been overworked in the last few days, Schwarzenberg proceeded to rest it about Troyes till the 10th. There we will leave it for the present whilst we trace the course of Napoleon's celebrated manoeuvre against Blücher.

Here, at the close of the first marked episode of the new campaign, it will be well to consider generally events since Napoleon rejoined his army at Châlons. In the first place, there arises the question whether between the Marne and the Aube was the best place for the Emperor to concentrate his army, or

---

4. The order appears to have been issued by Barclay, on the ground that Seslawin commanded Russian light troops; but it was approved by Schwarzenberg.

whether he would not have done better, as Clausewitz thinks, to defend Paris indirectly from the neighbourhood of Dijon. On the whole, Weil seems to have the best of the argument when he points out that the Emperor could only have collected there a force very inferior to the army of Bohemia. He would, at the same time, have left open to Blücher the main road from Metz to Paris. Under these circumstances, there was every chance that Blücher would push on to Paris, which he would find unfortified, unprotected in the Emperor's absence, and full of enemies of Napoleon only too ready to receive the allies with open arms.

Napoleon knew that Blücher was his most dangerous and implacable enemy, who would not hesitate to advance on Paris when he saw his way thereby to bring about the Emperor's downfall. With Napoleon in the south-east opposed to Schwarzenberg, the latter would be practically acting as an immensely powerful flank guard to Blücher's march. Had the lines of Schwarzenberg's and Blücher's advances been reversed, it might have been different; for Schwarzenberg on the northern line, covered by Blücher on the southern, would probably not have dared to march on Paris, even if Austrian statecraft had allowed him to.

We assume, then, that Napoleon rightly proposed to attack the two allied armies in detail from Châlons, before they could unite. He was there a week too late for his purpose.

Here is what is said by a very able modern French critic: [5]

It is a matter of regret that he [Napoleon] had not arrived to take the command of his troops a week earlier. Then, neglecting entirely the main body of the army of Bohemia, he could have assembled, between Toul and Nancy, Victor and Marmont, have reinforced them with the troops of Ney and Mortier, have resumed the offensive with nearly 40,000 men against Blücher, and driven him beyond the Moselle, and even on to the Sarre, notwithstanding the assistance the Field Marshal might have

---

5. A. G. (Grouard), *Maximes de Napoléon*, p. 11.

received from the right wing of the army of Bohemia. Then, quit of Blücher, Napoleon, rallying Macdonald and his new formations between Bar-le-Duc and Châlons, would have turned against Schwarzenberg, whose position would have been all the more perilous the farther he had penetrated into the valleys of the Seine and the Marne. At the head of 60,000 men he [Napoleon] would have forced him [Schwarzenberg] to retire or, at the least, would have prevented his advance.

That puts the case in a nutshell, and it seems to us beside the mark to argue with Weil that the marshals, with more ability and co-operation, might have held back the enemy, so that he was still in the position above described on the 26th January. They had not done so, and, knowing them as he did, Napoleon had no great reason to expect them to do so. With all the work of various kinds he had to do in Paris, it was no doubt difficult for the Emperor to be at Châlons earlier; but that is another matter. He had lost his opportunity of preventing the junction of the allied armies.

When he found he was too late, he took the most natural and reasonable course in attacking the nearest troops of the enemy, those of Blücher, whom it was not unreasonable to suppose he might still be in time to defeat, or even to annihilate, before they received the full support of the army of Bohemia. It would not have been much good to try and cut off Yorck; for that general could easily have retreated before him, drawing him forward into a most dangerous position.

We have already dealt with the battles of Brienne and La Rothière, and the reasons why Napoleon fought the latter. The Austrians never meant it to be the victory Blücher would have wished. What their views were is very clearly shown by a letter written by the Emperor of Austria to Schwarzenberg on the 29th January. [6] It is worth translating in full; for, though the hand is the hand of Francis, the voice is clearly Metternich's.

---

6. Given by *Weil* (2. 354), who found it in the archives at Vienna.

Even after having retaken Joinville and driven the enemy back on Vitry, we ought not, so long as the enemy is at Châlons, to march from Bar-sur-Aube to Troyes. We must not forget that the enemy can, from the South of France, move against our left, where the allies have few men, and that it is very necessary to hold strongly the road which, in case of a check, would serve for retreat. It is, therefore, indispensable both not to advance, and also to take all eventual measures for a retrograde movement. If, regardless of common sense, the Emperor of Russia should pronounce in favour of the forward march, you will insist on the previous assembly of a council of war, and you can be certain that I shall support your ideas.

When his own sovereign could write such a letter, it seems almost a sufficient excuse for all Schwarzenberg's hesitations. Small wonder, too, that Blücher should be anxious to get away from such an atmosphere.

The separation of the armies is strongly condemned by Clausewitz, and probably by every other critic, on strategical grounds. Blücher could not, for the present, expect to assemble more than 60,000 men, and that number, against 40,000 or 50,000 under Napoleon, could not be certain of victory.

The Emperor's retreat on Troyes was scarcely molested, as it certainly might have been, seeing that the enemy held all the bridges of the Aube down to Dienville.

CHAPTER 4

Champaubert, Montmirail, and Vauchamps

Napoleon, as we have seen, had already on the 2nd February foreseen the probable separation of Blücher and Schwarzenberg after La Rothière, and begun to meditate a blow against the former. [1] He was now in a position analogous to that he had hoped to hold at Châlons on the 26th January. The question was whether he should strike first at Blücher or at Schwarzenberg. Clausewitz holds that he rightly chose Blücher, the more dangerous and determined enemy, who might take the opportunity of an attack on Schwarzenberg to advance direct on Paris. Blücher was, too, the weaker in numbers, whilst Schwarzenberg would, with his known indecision, be more easily contained by a force left for the purpose.

Before starting, the Emperor reorganized his army. The cavalry, under the general command of Grouchy, was formed into four corps [2] and the separate division of Defrance.

He created a new 7th Corps under Oudinot, composed of the two divisions of Leval and Pierre Boyer just arriving from Soult's army. To contain the Bohemian army, he left the 7th corps, Victor with the 2nd corps, Gérard's Reserve of Paris, and the 5th cavalry corps. Pajol and Allix were on the Yonne. Mortier, with two divisions of Old Guard at Nogent, was to mask

---

1. *Supra*, p. 43.

2. 1st (Bordesoulle), 2nd (St. Germain), 5th (Milhaud), and 6th (Kellermann). Defrance had four regiments of Guards of Honour and the 10th Hussars.

47

the Emperor's movement and be ready to follow it. No supreme command was created over the containing troops.

Under this scheme, Victor in the centre would defend the heights of Pont-sur-Seine and the passage at Nogent, retiring to the right bank and blowing up the bridges if the enemy advanced in great strength. Oudinot would form the right, and would be reinforced by Rottembourg, at present guarding the parks at Provins. He would also have under his orders Pajol's cavalry at Montereau, Allix at Sens, and a brigade (600) of cavalry shortly due at Bray. If Schwarzenberg marched on Sens and Pont-sur-Yonne, or if Victor was forced on to the right bank of the Seine, Oudinot would concentrate with Victor towards Montereau. The total force left to contain the army of Bohemia was about 39,000 strong.

The left group of the army was the striking force which Napoleon took against Blücher, consisting of Mortier (temporarily left behind), Marmont, Ney's two divisions of Young Guard, part of the cavalry of the Guard, the 1st cavalry corps, and Defrance's cavalry division, in all about 20,000 infantry and 10,000 cavalry.

Here we must summarize the movements, since La Rothière, of Blücher, Yorck, and Macdonald.

Blücher, by the 4th February, was marching on Sommesous, after capturing a large convoy on the Châlons-Arcis road; Yorck, meanwhile, had driven Macdonald back to and out of Châlons on the 5th February. On this day Blücher, convinced that Napoleon was not endeavouring to draw Macdonald to himself, decided on joining Yorck in an attempt to destroy that marshal. In the evening Blücher received Schwarzenberg's letter explaining his southward move. Inferring from that letter that Napoleon was likely to be drawn well away from himself, Blücher decided on a manoeuvre which would certainly be very risky if Napoleon was likely to be able to interfere with it.

Yorck was to pursue Macdonald directly by the great Paris road along the left bank of the Marne to Château-Thierry, and thence by the right bank to La Ferté-sous-Jouarre. There

Blücher, marching by the chord of the arc by the "little" Paris road, through Champaubert and Montmirail, might hope to anticipate Macdonald, and either to crush him between Yorck and the rest of the Silesian army, or else to compel him to seek by difficult crossroads to gain the Soissons-Paris road. But Blücher wanted to combine two incompatible objects.

In addition to the attack on Macdonald westwards, he wanted to wait for Kleist and Kapzewitch, expected shortly from the east. He decided to keep Olsufiew's weak corps with himself, as a link connecting Kleist and Kapzewitch with Sacken, who was to move on La Ferté-sous-Jouarre. By the 8th the position was this: Macdonald, fully alive to his danger, had passed the Marne at Château-Thierry, and sent on cavalry to secure the next crossing at La Ferté-sous-Jouarre. Yorck's advanced guard (Katzeler) was pressing Macdonald, but the main body was still far behind.

Sacken's main body was at Montmirail, with cavalry at Viels Maisons. Twelve miles behind him, at Etoges, was Olsufiew with about 4000 men. Blücher's headquarters were at Vertus, nine miles behind Olsufiew, and Kleist and Kapzewitch were yet another sixteen miles behind, at Châlons. Thus, on the evening of the 8th, Blücher's main column was scattered over a length of some forty-four miles, whilst Yorck was some twelve or fourteen miles north, separated from Sacken by almost impassable roads. Had Napoleon really been where Blücher believed, there was no serious risk in this dispersion, for Macdonald had only some 10,000 men.

Blücher, being unaware that Seslawin no longer watched the space between his left and Wittgenstein, the right-hand corps of the army of Bohemia beyond the Aube, naturally expected that any French movement in that space would be reported to him by the Cossacks. So little anxiety was there in the Silesian army that when, in the evening of the 8th, Karpow's Cossacks were driven back from Sézanne on Montmirail, Sacken considered it of no importance, and did not report it. Yet, that same evening, Marmont had his leading division in Sézanne, and Ney was behind him, between Villenauxe and Sézanne.

During the 9th Macdonald got safely across the Marne again at La Ferté-sous-Jouarre, where he with difficulty repelled an attack of Wassiltchikow with Sacken's cavalry. Yorck had abandoned the pursuit of Macdonald as hopeless at Dormans; the French marshal had gained too long a start.

On the evening of the 9th Blüchers position was as scattered as ever; for, though he had sent Olsufiew on to Champaubert, and had been joined at Vertus and Bergeres by Kleist and Kapzewitch, Sacken's advance towards La Ferté-sous-Jouarre had equally lengthened the line at the western end.

During the day (9th) Marmont's cavalry, advancing northwards, had shown themselves as far forward as St. Prix on the Petit Morin, and even towards Champaubert. Even this created no alarm at Blücher's headquarters; for the very fact that this cavalry subsequently retired tended to allay the suspicion, which Müffling says he expressed, that it was the advanced guard of a large force. Blücher was still enjoying his fancied security without any suspicion of the storm gathering on his left.

Gneisenau, according to Müffling, would have nothing to do with the latter's inferences from the appearance of French cavalry, or his proposal to recall Sacken. The most Gneisenau would agree to was that Sacken should be told to remain at Montmirail, whence, if there was any serious movement of the enemy, he could either return to Blücher or join Yorck and pass the Marne at Château-Thierry, with a view to joining Winzingerode, who was now approaching from the north. In the former case there would be 39,000 men (Sacken, Olsufiew, Kleist, and Kapzewitch) towards Etoges, and 18,000 (Yorck) at Château-Thierry. In the other case there would be 38,000 (Sacken and Yorck) at Château-Thierry, and 19,000 about Etoges.[3]

At this juncture there arrived a letter from Schwarzenberg requesting Blücher to send Kleist to reinforce Wittgenstein on the right of the army of Bohemia. Consequently, Kleist and

---

3. The figures are Müffling's. He puts Sacken at 20,000, though Janson says he had only 16,000 at Montmirail.

Kapzewitch were ordered to march, on the 10th, on Sézanne, whither also Olsufiew would go from Champaubert.

Napoleon reached Sézanne late in the night of the 9th with the Guard. There had been immense difficulty in getting the guns over the terrible roads and marshes of the forest of Traconnes. The weather, which throughout this campaign was alternately freezing and thawing, was just now in the latter stage. But for the assistance of the peasants and their horses, the task would have been almost insuperable.

During the night of the 9th-10th Blücher at last learnt that Napoleon himself was with the troops at Sézanne. What was the Emperor going to do? Would he attack Olsufiew; or would he, disregarding this small Russian corps, make straight for Sacken by Montmirail? Was he only seeking to join Macdonald at La Ferté-sous-Jouarre? Blücher knew not. Sacken had been left some discretion as to what he would do. Müffling, according to his own account, sent one of his staff officers to try and persuade Sacken to exercise his discretion by marching on Champaubert. Gneisenau, however, stopped this officer, and changed his message to one telling Sacken that, if he still thought the repulse of Karpow's Cossacks on the 8th was unimportant, he should continue his pursuit of Macdonald. When the news of Napoleon's presence arrived it was too late to countermand this order.

Blücher now set off from Champaubert to join Kleist and Kapzewitch in their march to Sézanne. As they marched, in the morning of the 10th, they heard the roar of guns on their right, in the direction of Champaubert, but it was only in the afternoon that Blücher heard of the disaster which they heralded.

The "little" Paris road, along which Blücher's main column was spread, runs from Bergeres westwards along the southern edge of the undulating plateau which extends between the Marne on the north and the great marsh of St. Gond and the Petit Morin stream on the south. The road runs far enough from the edge to pass round the heads of the lateral valleys, which, especially about Champaubert and Montmirail, cut back into the plateau. On the Sézanne-Epernay road, on which Napoleon stood, the Petit Morin is crossed, just west of the St. Gond marsh, by a bridge at St. Prix. Over that bridge Olsufiew would have to pass on his march to Sézanne; therefore, he had not destroyed it. But he had also taken no measures to guard it, so that, when Napoleon sent forward his cavalry in the early morning of the 10th, it seized the passage unopposed.

Olsufiew had about 4000 [4] infantry and 24 guns, but no cavalry. He was, therefore, not in a position to fight Napoleon, and he should clearly have retreated towards Etoges. But he was smarting under censures for his mistake in letting the French capture the chateau at Brienne on the 29th January, and for his management of his troops at La Rothière. Sacken had even threatened him with a court-martial. Therefore, he resolved to stand when he heard of the French advance. He sent Udom with four regiments of infantry and six guns to hold Baye, about halfway between St. Prix and Champaubert.

Napoleon's cavalry was followed by Marmont and Ney. About 11 a.m. Ricard attacked Udom and drove him into Baye and the neighbouring woods, whilst Lagrange bore to the left towards Bannay. Olsufiew had now sent another brigade to support Udom, but Ney was soon up and firing with his artillery on Bannay, from which Lagrange's first attack had been repulsed.

By 3 p.m., after a stubborn resistance, both Baye and Bannay had been cleared of Russians. On the French right Bordessoulle's cavalry, on the left Doumerc's were pushing forward to cut off the Russian retreat.

Olsufiew, who had hitherto obstinately refused to retreat, though he had sent news to Blücher of what was happening, now attempted to fall back. Poltoratzki, with two regiments and nine guns, was left to hold Champaubert to the last, whilst Olsufiew, who had already sent off some of his guns, endeavoured to follow them to Etoges.

Poltoratzki, now surrounded by infantry, was charged on all sides by French cavalry. He made a brave resistance, and only

---

4. Poltoratzki told Napoleon he had only 3690. *Danilewski*, p. 106 (English translation).

surrendered, with 1000 men and nine guns, when his ammunition gave out.

Olsufiew, unable to get along the main road, took a side track through the woods towards Epernay; but, in the terrible weather on a wretched road, only about 1600 or 1700 men and fifteen guns succeeded in escaping through the woods. Olsufiew himself was captured.

Napoleon's victory was as complete as might have been expected from his great superiority of numbers.

The Emperor now stood in the midst of Blüchers widely separated corps. To the east were Kleist and Kapzewitch, now, on the receipt of news of Olsufiew's disaster, making a night march back to Vertus. They had already got nearly to Fère Champenoise when Blücher turned them back. Due west of Napoleon was Sacken, who had made matters worse by continuing his march on Trilport. Yorck was north-west at Château-Thierry and Viffort.

There could be little doubt as to the direction Napoleon would take. A movement against Blücher could only result in his retreat on Châlons or Epernay, whilst Yorck and Sacken escaped over the Marne at Château-Thierry.

If, however, the Emperor marched westwards against Sacken's rear, whilst Macdonald again advanced from Trilport, there was every possibility of annihilating Sacken, though Yorck might get away over the Marne. That, therefore, was the direction Napoleon chose.

Blücher, meanwhile, had written to Yorck to advance on Montmirail. The bridge at Château-Thierry, if restored, was to be kept open, "in order that, if unfortunately the enemy should cut your corps and Sacken's from my army, you may be able to escape to the right bank of the Marne." These orders only reached Yorck at night on the 10th.

To Sacken Blücher wrote merely that, concentrating with Yorck at Montmirail, he should be able to open the road to Vertus, if the enemy were between him and Blücher. Nothing was said to him about an escape over the Marne.

Napoleon had written, at 3 p.m., to Macdonald announcing his victory over Olsufiew, and telling him to move eastwards. At 7 p.m. he ordered Nansouty, with two divisions of cavalry, supported by two of Marmont's brigades, to seize Montmirail and reconnoitre towards Viels Maisons.[5] Mortier, now at Sézanne, was to march at daybreak for Montmirail, leaving a rear-guard at Suzanne and sending Defrance to get into touch with Leval's division which Oudinot had been ordered to send towards La Ferté Gaucher, [6] Leval, on reaching La Ferté Gaucher, was to march to the sound of the guns, which he would probably hear between Viels Maisons and Montmirail. Ney was to march, at 6 a.m., on Montmirail. Marmont to send Ricard at 3 a.m. to support Nansouty. He was himself to remain at Etoges, with Lagrange's division and the 1st Cavalry Corps, watching Blücher, and endeavouring to ascertain whether he was retreating on Châlons or Epernay, or contemplated the offensive westwards on Napoleon's rear.[7]

Of Napoleon's two prospective opponents, Yorck replied to Blücher's order of 7 a.m., saying that, if Napoleon's offensive movement continued, his own junction with Sacken seemed impossible. He had no information as to Sacken's intentions, and, as his own troops were too exhausted to move that night, he proposed to concentrate them next day at Viffort, with cav-

5. So spelt on the modern map. One would have expected Vieilles Maisons. Napoleon calls it Vieux Maisons.

6. Oudinot was also to send Rottembourg's division if he was not hard pressed. He was unable to do so.

7. Having issued his orders, Napoleon wrote to Joseph a ridiculously exaggerated account of his victory. A great deal of nonsense has been written about Napoleon's bulletins. He made no pretence that they were true, and, as in the case of this letter (*Corr.* 21,217), they were often deliberately exaggerated for political or military purposes. He has very frankly stated his views on this subject in another letter to Joseph (*Corr.* 21,360, dated 24th February, 1814). "Newspapers are no more history than bulletins are history. One ought always to make the enemy believe one has immense forces." Unless report lies, the Bulgarians of today have gone one better than Napoleon in encouraging the spread of reports of pursuits and actions which never took place at all. The author, for one, does not see that they or Napoleon can be blamed if exaggerated, or even false statements thus published were calculated to deceive the actual or possible enemy. In such matters, commanders can hardly be expected to adhere to a very severe standard of truth.

alry out towards Montmirail. Sacken, on the other hand, started on his return journey to Montmirail at 9 p.m. on the 10th, after again breaking the bridge at La Ferté-sous-Jouarre. It took him twelve hours to get to Viels Maisons, his advanced guard being in contact with the French farther east. Yorck was, at the same hour (9 a.m. on the 11th), at Viffort.

His cavalry had encountered French cavalry at Rozoy and Fontenelle. Knowing that Karpow's Cossacks had been driven from Montmirail in the early morning, and that Sacken had lost one possible line of retreat by destroying the bridge at La Ferté-sous-Jouarre, Yorck realized more clearly than Sacken the latter's danger. He sent to urge Sacken's immediate retreat on Château-Thierry. His staff officer found the Russian preparing for battle with what he persisted in calling only a weak detachment. He was unaffected by the information that Yorck could not reach the field till late, and even then without his heavy artillery, which the badness of the roads compelled him to leave at Château-Thierry with a brigade of infantry.

When Napoleon reached Montmirail, in the night of the 10th-11th, he was ignorant of the fact that Macdonald, by destroying the Trilport bridge, had put out of his own power that advance on Sacken's rear which Napoleon fully expected. The Emperor was satisfied, by an early reconnaissance, that Sacken and Yorck were still separated. Nansouty had already driven Russian outposts from Les Chouteaux farm, half-way to Viels Maisons. In order to prevent the union of Sacken and Yorck, the Emperor decided to take post at the junction of the road from Chateau-Thierry with the main road.

In those days it was between Le Tremblay and Montmirail, where a bye-road now comes in. Nansouty was across the Château-Thierry road short of le Plenois farm, with his artillery on his left, extending to the La Ferté road; Friant's Old Guard stood at the junction of the roads, with Defrance on his right. Mortier had not yet reached Montmirail.[8] This disposition shows that Napoleon expected an attack north of the La Ferté road, which,

8. He marched by the crossroad direct from Sézanne to Montmirail.

indeed, Sacken's staff urged on the ground of proximity to Yorck. But Sacken seems to have thought he could break a way past the "weak detachment" by the valley of the Petit Morin.

Tscherbatow's corps [9] was sent against Marchais, with Liewen's corps between it and the road. The cavalry alone was north of the road. Most of the heavy artillery was in the centre.

Sacken had about 16,300 men and 90 guns.[10] Napoleon, according to Houssaye had only 12,800. The highest accounts give him 20,000.

It was about 11 a.m. when Ricard was driven from Marchais. An hour later, more French artillery having come up in the interval, Napoleon sent him to retake the village, Friant moving up to Tremblay where Ricard had been. Mortier now replaced Friant at the cross roads.

At Marchais a furious combat raged till 2 p.m., the original 2300 Russians who had taken it being constantly reinforced. The French failed to retake it finally by this hour. Napoleon now sent Ney forward, covered on his right by Nansouty, on La Haute Epine north of the road.

This attack fell upon Sacken's left which he had weakened in order to strengthen the force towards Marchais. Ney broke through the first line and the fight was only restored by the use of Russian reserves. Nansouty, meanwhile, had been brought to a standstill by Wassiltchikow's cavalry, now in touch on its left with that of Yorck. Then Guyot charged with four squadrons of the Emperor's personal Guard. Charging past La Haute Epine, simultaneously occupied by Friant, Guyot broke up some Russian infantry trying to cross the road northwards.

Sacken's centre was now seriously shaken, his left, still in Marchais, in great danger.

We must now see what Yorck had been doing. Finding that Sacken was determined to fight, he first safeguarded his own

9. Commanded by Talisin II., *vice* Tscherbatow sick.
10. The number is given by Janson, but Müffling says Sacken had 20,000. He had 26,500 in the beginning of January: he had lost perhaps 5500 at Brienne and La Rothière. Sacken had 13,679 men left on the 16th February, and, as his losses on the nth and 12th were about 4300, he should have had 18,000 at Montmirail,

retreat by sending back another brigade to Château-Thierry. He feared an attack by Macdonald on his right and rear. His two remaining brigades (Horn and Pirch) could only reach Fontenelle over the sodden road at 3.30 p. m. Katzeler's cavalry had already joined Wassiltchikow against Nansouty. The Prussian reserve cavalry now deployed between Fontenelle and Les Tournaux, as did the infantry. As they advanced on Plenois and Bailly they were met by Mortier with Michel's division, who, after a stubborn fight, drove them back on Fontenelle where night brought the fighting to an end. Sacken was in great danger of being completely surrounded; for Napoleon, reinforcing the attack on Marchais, at last took the village. Its defenders, charged by Defrance as they left it, were nearly all killed or taken.

Nevertheless, Yorck's timely intervention had gained time for the débris of Sacken's corps to get away by their left to join him on the Château-Thierry road.

In their short combat with Michel the Prussians had lost about 900 men. Sacken naturally lost more heavily, altogether about 2000 killed and wounded, 800 prisoners, six standards, and thirteen guns. The French loss was about 2000 killed and wounded. They were too exhausted to pursue that night.

Blücher, with Kleist and Kapzewitch, had got back to Bergeres on the morning of the 11th. As he had no cavalry for the moment, he proposed retreating through the wooded country towards Epernay, rather than over the open plain to Châlons.

Receiving Yorck's message of the previous night,[11] he at once despatched orders to him and Sacken to cross the Marne and make for Reims, where the army would reassemble. When Yorck received this, he had just heard Sacken was moving by his right instead of his left. He felt bound to try and rescue the Russians.

Macdonald, receiving at Meaux the order to advance, found himself unable, owing to his own destruction of the Trilport bridge, to do more than send St. Germain's cavalry round by Lagny and Coulommiers, promising to follow by the same road next day. St. Germain reached Napoleon after the battle; Sebas-

11. *Supra*, p. 62.

tiani, who had tried to get over by La Ferté-sous-Jouarre, was held up by the broken bridge.

The French pursuit of Sacken and Yorck only started again at 9 a.m. on the 12th, Mortier by the direct road, the Emperor through Haute Epine and Rozoy.

The Prussians covering Sacken's retreat made some stand at Les Caquerets and again in front of Château-Thierry, but on each occasion they were forced back, and at the last place Ney, defeating the cavalry on their left, arrived on the heights overlooking the Marne. The Prussian infantry with difficulty escaped, and Heidenreich, on their right, was compelled to surrender with two Russian regiments. Finally, the passage of the Marne was only effected in safety thanks to the fire of a heavy battery from beyond the river.

This day cost the Prussians about 1250 men, six guns, and part of their baggage, whilst Sacken lost 1500 men, three guns, and nearly all his wheeled transport. The French loss did not exceed 600. Mortier was detailed for the pursuit of Sacken and Yorck with Christian's Old Guard division and the cavalry of Colbert and Defrance. It was only on the afternoon of the 13th that the bridge could be restored for his passage. By that time, Yorck and Sacken were far away at Fismes.

Napoleon spent the night of the 12th-13th at Château-Thierry. Believing that Oudinot and Victor were still holding Schwarzenberg at Nogent, and that Blücher had retreated either on Châlons or Epernay, he ordered, (1) Ricard to march from Montmirail to rejoin Marmont, (2) Macdonald to amalgamate his own (9th) corps and Sebastiani's (5th) into one (11th), and to be ready to march with it, reinforced by a National Guard division just arrived at Meaux from Paris.

At 2 p.m. news of the advance of Schwarzenberg decided the Emperor to leave the Silesian army and return to the Seine. Macdonald was to march for Montereau, where Napoleon hoped to have 27,000 infantry and 10,000 cavalry by the 15th. But news presently arrived from Marmont which showed that a blow must be struck at Blücher first. The Prussian Field Marshal had not retreated; for Marmont, with only 2500 infantry and 1800 cavalry, had not dared to molest him. His inactivity at last induced Blücher to believe that Napoleon was off to the Seine, with Marmont covering his march to Sézanne. On the evening of the 12th, Blücher decided to attack Marmont next day, hoping then to descend on Napoleon's rear as the Emperor marched for the Seine. He had now got some 800 cavalry.

Marmont, at Etoges, at once recognized that he could not make head even against Ziethen's advanced guard of 5000 infantry and 700 cavalry. By night on the 13th, Blücher's headquarters were at Champaubert, with Ziethen in front of him, and Kleist and Kapzewitch behind. Marmont had retired in good order to Fromentières.

It was 3 a.m. on the 14th when Napoleon heard of Blücher's advance. He at once ordered to advance east of Montmirail Ney, St. Germain, Friant, Curial, and Leval, the last named having only reached Viels Maisons the previous evening. The Emperor said he hoped to be at Montmirail in person by 7 a.m. and to give Blücher a lesson by noon. A good position was to be chosen east of Montmirail.

At 4.30 a.m. Marmont had begun to fall back.

Blücher only moved two hours later. There was a little skirmishing with Ziethen before Marmont got through Vauchamps, behind which village he drew up the 5000 men he had since Ricard had rejoined. His left was thrown forward into a small wood. At 10 a.m. Ziethen attacked with his Prussian infantry on the right, the cavalry on their left, and 3000 Russian infantry on the left rear of it.

Blücher, starting three hours after Ziethen, was only at Fromentières when he learnt that there was French infantry in the wood of Beaumont and cavalry north of the road, threatening to push in between Ziethen and himself. Marmont, with the Emperor's reinforcements now coming up, sent Ricard forward with the 800 men who were all that now remained of his division. Ziethen at first repulsed him, but then, as he pursued, was attacked by Lagrange in front and by cavalry on his right

The latter was Grouchy's which the Emperor had sent round by Sarrechamps. Ziethen was disastrously defeated, only 532 men out of four Prussian battalions escaping to Janvilliers. The Russian infantry retreated in squares in good order. Kleist and Kapzewitch, meanwhile, had only reached Fromentières at noon, where they heard the sound of Ziethen's fight. Hacke's 2000 cavalry, which had reached

Blücher on the 13th, was sent forward, whilst the infantry deployed across the road a mile east of Vauchamps. Blücher now saw Grouchy's cavalry moving in great strength round his right. His inference that Napoleon was present was confirmed by a French prisoner. With his line of retreat threatened by Grouchy, he decided to fall back on Etoges. The road was reserved for guns and wagons, whilst the infantry, with only a few guns, marched over the sodden fields, Kleist north, Kapzewitch south of the road. Udom, with the remains of Olsufiew's corps, had been left at Champaubert, and was now ordered to hold the great wood of La Grande Laye, between that place and Etoges.

At first the retreat progressed in good order, though harassed by constant attacks by Grouchy's cavalry on the north, and the Guard cavalry on the south.

Müffling, marching with Kleist, was hurrying the retreat of the right in order to seize the defile between La Grande Laye and the large pond. Kleist was thus some way ahead of Kapzewitch, who was more harassed by the French infantry in front, and by cavalry charges. Blücher, who was with Kapzewitch, now ordered Kleist to wait for him. By this time Grouchy was up to La Grande Laye which, under orders from Kapzewitch, Udom had evacuated in order to retreat on Etoges. At 4.30 Grouchy advanced south- westwards in four long lines between La Grande Laye and the Champaubert-Epernay road.

Carrying away Hacke's cavalry, he fell upon Kleist's infantry, which was simultaneously charged by Laferrière's Guard cavalry on its left. Assailed in front, flank, and rear, with many of his squares broken, Kleist's plight seemed desperate. It was only by immense personal exertions on the part of Blücher, Müffling,

Kleist, and others that the men were rallied and a way was forced through Grouchy's cavalry to Etoges. Had Grouchy's horse artillery not been kept back by the clayey soil, Kleist could hardly have escaped at all. Blücher again narrowly escaped capture.

Night having now fallen, Ney rallied his cavalry and sent only a portion of it after the enemy as they retreated. Blücher's remaining troops were utterly exhausted. Nevertheless, the old marshal decided to continue his retreat on Châlons at once, leaving only Ouroussow's division in Etoges to cover the retreat. Fighting seemed over for the day. Ouroussow's men were dispersed in Etoges, hunting for food and fuel, and keeping no lookout, when once more the French fell on them. Napoleon, already on his way back to Montmirail with Ney, the Guard, and Leval, had sent orders to Marmont to follow on Blücher's heels. It was between 8 and 9 p.m. when Marmont's troops surprised Ouroussow.

The attack was made with the bayonet on men who had mostly laid aside their arms in the search for food. All but a very few were killed, wounded, or taken, Ouroussow amongst the latter. This day (14th February) had been almost more disastrous than its predecessors for Blücher's army. The Prussians lost about 4000 men and seven guns, nearly half Kleist's strength. Kapzewitch lost over 2000 men and nine guns. The French loss was again insignificant, being estimated at only 600. In the four days' fighting at Champaubert, Montmirail, Château-Thierry, and Vauchamps, Blücher's army of about 56,000 men had lost over 16,000 men and forty-seven guns. Napoleon's loss had been only about 4000.

This is a convenient place for reviewing generally Napoleon's manoeuvre against Blücher, which is considered, rightly probably, to be the finest he made in 1814. His conduct has been praised to the sky, whilst Blücher has been blamed equally. Both praise and blame seem to be excessive. To begin with Napoleon, the idea of an attack on Blücher whilst Schwarzenberg was contained on the Seine was exactly what might have been expected from the great master of operations on interior lines, from the commander of the French army in Italy in 1796. The way in which he masked his march from Schwarzenberg, the rapidity of its execution in the face of fearful difficulties of roads, were worthy of Napoleon's best days, and of the pluck and tenacity of his soldiers.

Neither Blücher nor Schwarzenberg realized what was happening till the Emperor fell like a thunderbolt on the hapless Olsufiew. Yet Napoleon owed much, in his escape from the notice of Blücher, to luck, or rather to the mistakes of his opponents. Blücher still believed, up to the 9th February, that Seslawin was watching the country between his left and the Aube. Had that been so, Seslawin should have been able to report Napoleon's march. Blücher must certainly be blamed in part for his ignorance of Seslawin's departure. Of course he ought to have been informed of it, but, on the other hand, he would have done better to keep himself in touch with Seslawin through a staff officer deputed to the latter's head-quarters. [12] This want of intercommunication between commandants of corps was one of the marked defects of the allied command.

When Napoleon fell upon Olsufiew, the army of Silesia was scattered in isolated corps over an immense distance. This was due to Blücher's endeavour to compass two separate and incompatible objects:

(1) the destruction of Macdonald, and

(2) the rallying to himself of Kleist and Kapzewitch. For the dispersion of his army Blücher has been greatly blamed. But it must be remembered in his favour that he had good reason to believe himself safe from any movement of Napoleon against himself.

That belief was based on his assumption that Seslawin was still watching between himself and the Aube, and on Schwarzenberg's statements as to Napoleon's supposed intention of moving farther south. In that case, the Emperor would have been far

---

12. On this subject see Captain Jones' lectures on this campaign.

out of reach of Blücher, and there would have been no risk in the separation of the corps, with only such a weak opponent as Macdonald before them. Either Yorck or Sacken alone was more than a match for him.

On the other hand, critics after the event seem to have considered that Napoleon knew before he started that he would find Blücher's army scattered as it was. He knew nothing of the sort, and it was probably only at Champaubert that he realized how wonderfully lucky he had been in coming on the centre of a long line, instead of finding his 30,000 men opposed to a concentrated army of over 50,000.

Blücher's march with Kleist and Kapzewitch on Fère Champenoise on the 10th, a march which still continued to the accompaniment of the guns at Champaubert, is condemned even by Clausewitz, who is little inclined to find fault with Blücher. Perhaps Blücher believed that the movement towards his right rear would stop Napoleon; but more weight may probably be given to his habitual loyalty and his desire to move Kleist as ordered by Schwarzenberg. Olsufiew certainly made a grievous mistake in deciding to fight a hopeless battle at Champaubert, and in refusing to retreat, though urged to do so by Blücher's *aide-de-camp*, Nostitz, and his own generals, until it was too late. We have already alluded to the fear of censure which influenced a general of little capacity.

Napoleon, after Champaubert, was in a thoroughly congenial position. Little credit need be given him for marching against Sacken whilst Marmont watched Blücher. It was a course obviously right even to smaller men than the Emperor. Sacken sinned, like Blücher and Olsufiew, in obstinately refusing to attribute its true importance to Napoleon's advance on Montmirail till it was too late. He insisted on advancing towards his right, instead of bearing to his left towards Yorck.

Gneisenau, however, should have warned him, as he did warn Yorck, of the possibility of a retreat across the Marne being necessary. As it was, his movement to the right played into the hands of Napoleon, whose design was to cut him from Yorck. Sacken had much to be thankful for that he effected an almost miraculous escape in the end. Müffling says he had only a forest road by which to reach Yorck, and that he only got his artillery along by hitching on cavalry horses. He owed the possibility of escape mainly to Yorck's timely intervention on Napoleon's right. On the other hand, Yorck might perhaps have done more towards helping Sacken. Had they united in time to meet Napoleon they would have had a great advantage in numbers. Blücher did nothing against Marmont on the 11th or 12th February, which seems difficult to explain, except on the ground of his want of cavalry, of which he only got 800 on the 12th and 2000 more on the 13th.

His advance on the latter date was due to his belief that Marmont was merely the rearguard of Napoleon's march by Sézanne to the Seine. He, too, was very fortunate in escaping at Vauchamps, an escape which was probably due mainly to Grouchy being unable to bring up his artillery, and perhaps to some slackness in the French infantry pressure on his front. Kapzewitch certainly made matters worse by his unwarranted order to Udom to retreat from La Grande Laye on Etoges. Had Grouchy found Udom's 1500 men in the wood, instead of only a few skirmishers on its edge, he would have been greatly hampered in his attack on Kleist.

Napoleon's movement against Blücher was a brilliant success, but by no means so complete as he hoped for. He started with the hope of annihilating the army of Silesia before returning to the Seine. He had inflicted losses on it amounting to between one-fourth and one-third of its strength, but he had certainly not annihilated it.

When it had been two days (16th-18th February) at Châlons, and been reinforced by 6000 Russian infantry, 2000 of Korff's cavalry and other bodies, it was ready to march again, 53,000 strong, as if it had never been defeated at all.

Blücher was always hopeful and plucky. On the 13th, before Vauchamps, he wrote to his wife, in a letter full of misspellings,

"I have had a bitter three days. Napoleon has attacked me

three times in the three days with his whole strength and all his Guard, but has not gained his object, and today he is in retreat on Paris. Tomorrow I follow him, then our army will unite, and in front of Paris a great battle will decide all. Don't be afraid that we shall be beaten; unless some unheard-of mistake occurs, that is not possible." [13]

---

13. *Janson*, 1., note 139 (at end of volume).

CHAPTER 5

Napoleon Returns to the Seine

It was high time, when Napoleon had defeated Blücher at Vauchamps, for him to hurry to the assistance of his containing force on the Seine.

Schwarzenberg had only resumed his advance from Troyes on the 10th February, the day of Olsufiew's disaster.

Wittgenstein and Wrede moved against Nogent and Bray. Würtemberg was to move on Sens, with Bianchi [1] on his left. These two were to be supported by Gyulai, whilst the Guards and Reserves moved towards Méry in support of the two corps on the right

Next day Victor retired behind the Seine, leaving only a rearguard on the left bank at Nogent. Würtemberg drove Allix out of Sens and across the Seine at Montereau.

During the succeeding days the Austrians of Bianchi pushed as far forward as the Loing, and even to Fontainebleau. Victor's rearguard made a good fight at Nogent on the 12th, but eventually crossed the river and destroyed the bridge. Schwarzenberg, now hearing of Olsufiew's defeat, sent Diebitsch with cavalry to take the place of connecting link with Blücher lately occupied by Seslawin. Barclay's Guards were to concentrate at Méry.

Wittgenstein and Wrede now got across the Seine, thanks to Wrede's capture of Bray from its weak garrison of National Guards, which was the event that compelled Victor to retire and blow up the Nogent bridge.

---

1. Now commanding the 1st Corps *vice* Colloredo wounded.

When Wrede was across at Bray, he came into collision with Oudinot, whom he failed to defeat on the 13th. Oudinot and Victor, however, retired in the night to Nangis. The former, who had sent Leval's veterans to Napoleon, had urgently demanded reinforcements. To this demand Napoleon had responded by his order of the 13th, directing Macdonald on Montereau. [2] That marshal now, thanks to reinforcements from Paris, at the head of 12,000 men, reached Guignes on the evening of the 14th. On the 15th the general line of French defence was the river Yeres. A glance at the map will show how painfully near that was to Paris; indeed, the capital had already been panic-stricken by a mistaken order which resulted in the trains going behind the Marne close to Paris.

It will be remembered that Caulaincourt had been summoned to the Congress of Châtillon-sur-Seine on the 3rd February. The allies, flushed with the victory of La Rothière, had raised their terms, and now insisted on the confinement of France within her frontiers of 1789. Indeed, the Tsar appears to have told Lord Castlereagh that he would not make peace whilst Napoleon remained on the throne. The negotiations, after a great deal of fencing, the details of which are foreign to this history, were suspended on the 10th February.

The news of Vauchamps and the other defeats of the army of Silesia induced even the Tsar to consider matters in a different light, whilst Napoleon was encouraged to hope for the terms of Frankfort at least. The Congress eventually resumed its sittings on the 17th February. Napoleon had other matters to consider besides the army of Bohemia, against which he was now about to march, and that of Silesia which he erroneously believed to be crippled for some time at least.

Winzingerode had at last dragged his corps forward as far as Soissons, which was stormed on the 14th, but relinquished at once when Winzingerode marched by Epernay to Reims.

Bülow also, the Emperor learned, showed signs of marching southwards.

2. *Supra*, p. 67.

Accordingly, Napoleon sent orders to Maison in the Netherlands to avoid locking up his army in the fortresses, so as to be able with it in the open field to keep Bülow there. Mortier was to fix his line of operations on the Paris–Soissons road, so as to be prepared to meet an advance by Winzingerode or Bülow. Marmont was to keep Blücher back towards Châlons, and only to retreat slowly on Montmirail and Sézanne if seriously threatened.

The Emperor's optimism had been so stimulated by his successes that he now again contemplated the possibility of retaining his hold on Italy, and urged Eugene to activity.

Lastly, he now saw his way to alarming Schwarzenberg for his communications, by using Augereau's forces in the south against Bubna and Hessen Homburg who guarded the left rear of the army of Bohemia. Augereau was now at the head of some 27,000 men towards Lyons. Of these about 12,000 were excellent troops, mostly drawn from Suchet's army. The rest were National Guards and other troops of smaller value. Napoleon urged Augereau to go straight for Hessen Homburg by Macon and Châlons-sur-Saone. We shall see presently that this threat had important consequences, though Augereau's conduct was generally feeble. He appears never to have made up his mind "to pull on his boots of 1793" as Napoleon, in his vigorous letter of the 21st February, urged him to do. [3]

Such was the general situation in France during the few days succeeding Vauchamps.

Napoleon was at La Ferté-sous-Jouarre on the 15th February, at Guignes on the evening of the 1 6th, bringing with him at express speed all the troops he had, except those left behind with Mortier and Marmont.

Orders issued at 1 a.m. on the 17th for an immediate general advance against Schwarzenberg.

That commander was now completely unnerved by the news of Blücher's disasters. The first view held at a council of war at Nogent had been that Blücher was being pursued towards

---

3. *Corr.* 21,343

Châlons by Napoleon, and that the best thing to be done was to move Wittgenstein and Wrede by Sézanne against the Emperor's rear, in order to relieve the pressure on Blücher, and at the same time to cover the retreat of the army of Bohemia, and its concentration on Arcis-sur-Aube and Troyes. Before that movement had Napoleon really begun came news from Blücher that, after Vauchamps, Napoleon had fallen back, and was apparently moving against the army of Bohemia.

The only thought now was how to get the army back behind the Seine and the Yonne, under the covering protection of Wrede, Wittgenstein, and Barclay. Schwarzenberg's great idea was always to have a considerable river between himself and the dreaded enemy. Wittgenstein, as it was, had advanced a good deal farther than Schwarzenberg liked; for Pahlen with his advanced guard was at and beyond Mormant, close up to the front of the marshals, now about to be joined by the Emperor.

Wittgenstein was ordered to fall back on the 17th on Provins; Wrede to hold fast at Donnemarie, with an advanced guard towards Nangis keeping him in touch with Wittgenstein. Bray was indicated as the line of retreat of both corps. Barclay with the Russo-Prussian Guards and Reserves to assemble between Nogent and Pont-sur-Seine.

Diebitsch had already been sent with cavalry to Montmirail, into the position lately occupied by Seslawin, who was now far away on the left, nearly up to the gates of Orleans. Würtemberg and Bianchi were about Montereau, Gyulai at Pont-sur-Yonne, the Austrian reserves at Sens, and there were advanced guards towards Melun on the right bank of the Seine, at Fontainebleau, and Platow was at Nemours. It was necessary to hold the passage of the Seine and Yonne at Montereau, in order to cover the retreat of the corps on the left of the Bohemian army.

On the morning of the 17th Pahlen was attacked at Mormant by Gérard, leading Napoleon's advance, and outflanked on both wings by French cavalry. He was badly beaten, with a loss of 2000 men and ten guns as he retreated. At Nangis Wrede's advanced guard was driven back with heavy loss till it met a Bavarian brigade at Villeneuve-le-Comte. At Nangis Napoleon divided his pursuit, sending Victor with the 2nd corps, Gérard's Reserve of Paris, and L'Héritier's and Bordessoulle's cavalry to seize the passage at Montereau.

Oudinot on the left, with the 7th corps and Kellermann's cavalry, followed Wittgenstein towards Provins. Macdonald, with the 11th corps and two cavalry divisions, was the centre, with the Guard in reserve. Victor again attacked Wrede's advanced guard near Villeneuve (action of Valjouan), and drove it back on the main body of Wrede, who crossed the Seine at Bray during the night. Napoleon was furious that Victor did not press on to Montereau that evening. Pajol, during this day, advanced with his cavalry, and Pacthod's National Guards, driving Würtemberg's advanced guard back along the Melun-Montereau road to within five miles of the latter place. Charpentier and Allix were on the road to Fontainebleau from Melun.

The only really important fighting on the 18th took place at Montereau which, after several rather contradictory orders from Schwarzenberg, Würtemberg was told to hold at any rate till the night of the 18th.

When Oudinot advanced that evening, Wittgenstein had passed at Nogent, and Wrede was across at Bray, all but a rear-guard left at the defile of Mouy. Victor's orders were to be at Montereau by 6 a.m.

The passage of the Seine at Montereau was by a bridge which reached the left bank just above the inflow of the Yonne, over which also there was a bridge. The right bank of the Seine here commands the left, as one sees in passing by train from Dijon to Paris. The left bank is quite flat about Montereau, the right rises steeply 150 or 200 feet above the river, falling again towards the north.

The Crown Prince placed on the right bank about 8500 infantry, 1000 cavalry, and twenty-six guns. His left was in Villaron (Les Ormeaux) and the vineyards about it across the road to Paris, the centre held the *château* and park of Surville, and the plateau in front, the right extended to the road to Salins and the *château* of Courbeton. On the left bank of the Seine he had two Austrian batteries, one supporting each wing. In the eastern suburb of Montereau, and behind at the farm of Motteux, was the remaining brigade of the 4th corps. Bianchi, who was retiring by Pont-sur-Yonne, had left one brigade and the two batteries above mentioned, to help the Crown Prince.

Pajol was the first of the French to come up about 8 a.m. by the Paris road with 1500 cavalry, 3000 National Guards (Pacthod) and 800 *gendarmes* from Spain. The cavalry was almost untrained, and Pacthod's men only very in differently equipped and trained. Pajol was unable with his feeble troops to make any progress. At 9 a.m. Victor's leading troops failed in an attack on the enemy's left. It was not renewed, and all efforts were now concentrated on Villaron which covered the enemy's line of retreat.

Then there arrived Duhesme's division and General Chataux's. Both these were driven back from Villaron, and Chataux was mortally wounded. The Würtemberg cavalry made a vigorous counter attack, driving the French cavalry back to the woods. At 11 a.m. Victor, unable to make headway, was waiting for the arrival of Gérard. Victor was now superseded in command of the 2nd corps by Gérard, as a mark of the Emperor's displeasure at his slowness on the previous day.

It was 3 p.m. when Napoleon reached the field with the Guard. A fresh attack was now organized in four columns, of which three moved on Villaron and Surville, the fourth by the valley of the Seine against the allied right. Pajol's troops again moved forward against the left of Villaron. The Guard was in reserve. A heavy artillery fire was poured on the Surville chateau. Villaron was at last taken and Pajol fell upon the Würtembergers' left with his cavalry, just as the Crown Prince was commencing a retreat, which he saw to be inevitable in face of the 30,000 men and seventy guns now opposed to his small force.

Schaefer's brigade, in the park of Surville, was ordered to cover the retreat by the bridge, but the chateau was stormed and its defenders captured. The retreat now degenerated into a wild flight down the steep slopes towards the bridge. Pajol, charging along the main road, crossed the bridge over the Seine along with the fugitives, sabring them right and left, continuing over the Yonne bridge, and clearing Montereau completely of the enemy. The debris of the defeated brigades fell back on that of Hohenlohe, and the whole retired in confusion on La Tombe, covered by Jett's cavalry of Hohenlohe's brigade.

The battle of Montereau was a severe defeat for the allies, who lost nearly 5000 men, 3400 of them being prisoners, and fifteen guns. Moreover, it gave Napoleon the important bridges over the Seine and Yonne. For this he was mainly indebted to the magnificent energy of Pajol's last charge which converted the allied retreat into a rout, and left the enemy no time to blow up the bridges. Pajol was so badly wounded that he could take no further part in the war.

The Crown Prince and his troops made a gallant effort to resist overwhelming forces, which they kept in check for many hours; but their position, with the river spanned by only one bridge at their back, was one in which defeat was almost sure to be followed by disaster. They would probably have done the Emperor more harm by retreating at once and effectually blowing up the Seine bridge, but Schwarzenberg's orders forbade this course.

On this day the French reached the Seine at Nogent and Bray, but found the bridges destroyed at both places, which made the Montereau bridge of supreme importance, for Napoleon had no bridging equipment as yet. On the allied left the Austrian troops on and beyond the Loing fell back before Allix and Charpentier. When Montereau was taken, their position became very dangerous, and it was only by pretended negotiations with Allix that they gained time to retreat south-eastwards to rejoin the remains of the brigade which Bianchi had left behind at Montereau, and which had been forced up the left bank of the Yonne to Serotin.

On the extreme left, Seslawin, who was before Orleans, was once more ordered back to the opposite flank, to replace Diebitsch who crossed to the left bank of the Aube at Plancy.

Even before he was aware of what was happening at Montereau, Schwarzenberg had issued orders for a general retreat on Troyes, alleging as his object the avoidance of partial combats of isolated corps, and concentration for battle about Troyes. When he received news of the defeat at Montereau, he ordered Wrede, whom he reinforced with a Russian *cuirassier* division, to hold fast at Bray till the evening of the 19th.

At 3 a.m. on the 19th he wrote to Blücher saying that, owing to the loss of Montereau, he was obliged to hurry his retreat on Troyes, whence he proposed to resume the offensive. But for this purpose he depended on Blücher's joining Wittgenstein at Méry by the 21st. Blücher's answer, which reached Schwarzenberg in the evening of the 19th, promised that he would be there on the date named with 53,000 men and 300 guns.

Napoleon, finding it doubtful when he would be able to pass the Seine at Bray and Nogent, at first began to send everything by Montereau, except Gérard [4] who was to pass at Pont-sur- Seine when he could restore the bridge. Afterwards, when Macdonald, on Wrede's retreat, was able partially to restore the bridge at Bray, Oudinot, Kellermann, and Nansouty were sent across there, followed by Ney and the Old Guard. Macdonald also was to cross there.

We need not follow in detail the movements of both sides in the next day or two, for Napoleon had practically lost contact with the army of Bohemia.

By the evening of the 20th Blücher was about Arcis-sur-Aube, where he received an urgent order from Schwarzenberg to join Wittgenstein who was on both banks of the Seine at Méry. Blücher's first idea, when he left Châlons with his rapidly reorganized and reinforced army on the 18th, had been a fresh westward march, but, in reply to Schwarzenberg's call, he at once prepared on the 19th for the move on Méry.

---

4. Gérard's new command (2nd corps) now consisted of Duhesme's division and the two divisions (Dufour and Hamelinaye) of Reserve of Paris. Victor was restored to favour and given command of two newly formed Young Guard divisions (Charpentier and Boyer de Rebeval).

It appears clear that when Schwarzenberg urged Blücher to an immediate junction with Wittgenstein, and explained how in a battle in the direction of Méry they could be supported by Wrede and Barclay moving against the French right, he still firmly intended fighting a battle on the 21st or 22nd. In the night of the 20th his views were suddenly changed by a report from the Prince of Hessen Homburg giving alarming news of the advance of Augereau against Châlons-sur-Saône and Besançon, and of Dessaix and Marchand from Savoy against Geneva. In consequence of this, Bianchi was ordered to make forced marches by Châtillon to Dijon, taking with him the I corps and his own former division of Austrian reserves, to which more troops were added. By these measures the forces of the army of Bohemia against Napoleon would be reduced to about 90,000 men. Blücher had about 50,000, making altogether about 140,000 against the 75,000 of Napoleon. [5]

It was quite clear that Schwarzenberg must make up his mind either to fight a decisive battle with Napoleon, or to continue his retreat at once. The poor country in which he now was, [6] exhausted by the passage and repassage of armies, was quite incapable of supporting the great forces of the allies, who were already suffering much from hunger, bad clothing, and weather which was alternately snowy or rainy. In such circumstances, there could be no question of a defensive aiming at wearing out the Emperor.

On the other hand, Schwarzenberg found it difficult to make up his mind to fight. He had little short of 150,000 men, including Blücher's army, and Napoleon had about half that number. But defeat at the hands of the dreaded enemy was always possible, and the Emperor's numbers were greatly exaggerated in the reports, [7] and in the imagination of Schwarzenberg. The Austrian could not get out of his head the incalculable results of

5. That is the number under the Emperor's immediate control, exclusive of Allix's detachment on his right, and of Mortier and Marmont on his left.

6. It is known as "*Champagne Pouilleuse*"—"Barren Champagne."

7. Seslawin, on the 21st, reported that Napoleon had 82 regiments of cavalry and altogether 180,000 men! Seslawin was looked upon at headquarters as very reliable.

defeat, with his retreat threatened by Augereau from the south. He had really made up his mind to retreat on

Chaumont, perhaps on the plateau of Langres, but he dared not say so plainly in face of the views of the Tsar and the King of Prussia, at least until he had made some show of more energy. He accordingly issued orders for a general reconnaissance on the 22nd, by cavalry supported by infantry, all along his front. This he said was required to procure definite information as to the enemy's movements. The reconnaissance was only to commence at noon, and long before that hour Napoleon's advance put it out of the question. That morning Kellermann's cavalry drove back Pahlen from Mégrigny.

When Oudinot's infantry came up, the part of Méry on the left bank of the Seine was stormed, and the part beyond the river was also temporarily occupied by a brigade which, however, was driven out again. The Emperor, arriving at this juncture, quickly recognized the presence of the whole army of Silesia. He was now in contact with the allies all along his front, from Méry to in front of Troyes. Apparently a battle was imminent, and the Emperor proposed to attack the army of Bohemia with the bulk of his army whilst, with a small force of his veterans from Spain, he held Blücher at Méry, preventing his passage of the Aube and interference with the French left and rear.

During the day Wrede's cavalry was driven back by Milhaud on Oudinot's right, and there were also French cavalry successes against the allied left towards Villeneuve l'Archevêque.

That night Schwarzenberg issued orders for retreat behind the Seine, except in the case of the 3rd corps which would follow the left bank to Bar-sur-Seine. Wrede would cover the retreat by holding Troyes till the 24th with one division.

In the morning of the 23rd, before the sovereigns and Schwarzenberg started for Vendœuvre, a council was held. It was decided to send Prince Lichtenstein to propose an armistice, for which overtures had already been made to, but not accepted by, Napoleon. Lichtenstein seems to have told the Emperor a good deal more than was desirable as to the difficulties of the allied army, but Napoleon was fully alive to the risks of a battle with his great inferiority of numbers. In the end, he sent Lichtenstein back with a promise that an officer would be sent next day to negotiate an armistice. He quite saw through the allies' desire to hold him back by negotiations, as well as by the show of defence of the Seine on the 23rd.

He had already on the 21st made another attempt to detach Austria from the alliance, by writing to his father-in-law a letter in which he definitely proposed peace on the terms offered from Frankfort. [8] His views of the military situation on the 23rd are stated in a letter to Joseph. [9] He would, he said, be in Troyes in two hours. The allies were retiring on Vendœuvre, whither Blücher's forces were also making, leaving nothing in front of Marmont towards Sézanne.

It was desirable, therefore, that Mortier should return to Château-Thierry, so as to set Marmont free to act with the Emperor. Napoleon was wrong as to Troyes; for, owing to Wrede's resistance and threat to fire the town, it was only at 6 a.m. on the 24th that the French entered. He was also wrong as to Blücher, for that commander had sent Grolmann, on the 22nd, to try and persuade Schwarzenberg to fight. If he failed in that, he was to propose a fresh separation of the armies, with the object of Blücher's uniting with Winzingerode from Reims, and Bülow, now marching from Belgium.

To the latter course the Austrian agreed, though he soon repented of having done so. But it was then too late. Schwarzenberg's view was that Blücher should operate, when reinforced, against Napoleon's rear, so as to draw him away from the pursuit towards Langres. Blücher's views were quite different, and contemplated his own advance on Paris with the 100,000 men he would have when joined by Winzingerode and Bülow.

As promised by the Emperor, Flahault was sent next day to carry on negotiations for an armistice, but his instructions required insistence on preliminary conditions, amongst them

---

8. *Corr.* 21,344.

9. *Corr.* 21,356, 23rd February, 2 p.m.

the acceptance of the conditions of peace offered at Frankfort, which foredoomed the negotiations to failure.

The fact is that Napoleon was at this time suffering from an attack of the optimistic illusions which so often, in these later years, blinded him to actual facts. He painted his own situation in the rosiest, that of the enemy in the darkest of colours. He pictured to himself an enemy routed and retreating in the wildest disorder, which was very far from being the case. When Wrede threatened to burn Troyes if the French tried to storm it before the morning of the 24th, Napoleon, according to de Ségur, remarked, "Such affronts deserve to be washed out in blood. I will make the allies repent of their violence. They shall see that I am nearer to their capitals than they to mine."

Such vain boasts were unknown in earlier days. Then he only uttered threats on a well-weighed appreciation of actual facts; now he spoke hastily on presumptions and insufficient grounds. Formerly when he prophesied the course of military events he was rarely wrong; now his hasty prophecies were more often falsified than verified. He had recently avowed that Blücher had been destroyed; yet now the old marshal again faced him, as strong as ever. On the 24th he wrote to Joseph, [10]

Terror reigns in the ranks of the allies. A few days ago they believed I had no army; today there is nothing at which their imagination sticks; 300,000 or 400,000 men is not enough for them. They believed just now that I had nothing but recruits; today they say I have assembled all my veterans, and that I bring against them nothing but picked armies, that the French army is better than ever, etc., . . . such is their terror.

It is true that this was written for the benefit of Joseph and Paris, but it indicates the Emperor's frame of mind, and the little likelihood of his being prepared to negotiate in earnest.

An hour after Napoleon entered Troyes it was clear that the main body of Schwarzenberg's army was making for Bar-sur-

10. *Corr.* 21,360.

Aube by Vendœuvre; one column was moving by Piney, and another by the left bank of the Seine on Bar-sur-Seine. Of Blücher there was no news.

Orders for the pursuit issued at once; Gérard was to lead on the road to Vendœuvre with the 2nd corps and a strong cavalry force. Behind him was Oudinot, and Ney was to go as far as La Guillotière, in case he was required. Macdonald, with the 11th corps and Kellermann's and Milhaud's cavalry, was detailed to follow by the left bank of the Seine.

The rest of the army was moved up towards Troyes, except Bordessoulle, who was to try and communicate with Marmont from Anglure.

Napoleon committed himself to the statement that the whole of Blüchers force had crossed the Aube in order to join Schwarzenberg by a march along its right bank. That was merely an assumption, and quite a wrong one. It was proved to be so by the receipt of news from Pierre Boyer that, before he left Méry, he had seen Blücher moving in the opposite direction towards the lower Aube. That brought Napoleon back to Troyes with the Guard cavalry; for the movement seemed to aim at his communications.

The general arrangement of Napoleon's army on the night of the 24th was this. He had two strong advanced guards (Gérard and Macdonald) following the enemy on both banks of the Seine. Marmont and Bordessoulle were charged with the watch of Blücher. The main body of the army, about Troyes, formed a central reserve which could be sent in any direction required. By evening Gérard had got to between Lusigny and Vendœuvre after some fighting. Macdonald was at St. Parre les Vaudes, with cavalry towards Bar-sur-Seine. Marmont had started from Sézanne in order, as he says, [11] to approach the Aube, to support himself by the river, and to keep in touch with the Emperor.

At Pleurs he met Russian cavalry, and ascertained that Blücher had already crossed to the right bank of the Aube by his bridges at Plancy and Baudemont. Finding himself with only

11. *Mém.* 6. 197.

6000 men in front of Blücher, Marmont returned to Sézanne in the evening, and took post on the heights behind it. Bordessoulle also as he began, in accordance with Napoleon's orders, his advance on Anglure and Plancy, found the enemy in force at Marcilly, and fell back.

Blücher's army that night (24th) was spread along both banks of the Aube, from Plancy to its mouth.

As we know, Pierre Boyer had reported Blücher's move down the Aube. The question for Napoleon was what this meant. Was Blücher moving towards Paris? Was he retreating on Châlons? Or was he going to move up the right bank of the Aube to rejoin Schwarzenberg? The latter alternative certainly seemed unlikely, for why should Blücher move down the Aube when he intended to move up again by the opposite bank? If that was his intention, he could have crossed at Plancy and Arcis. The Emperor could not be sure regarding the other two alternatives till he heard from Bordessoulle and Marmont, from neither of whom had he received any report at 3 a.m. on the 25th when he had to issue orders for the day.

Yet, we would point out that it should hardly have seemed likely that Blücher was going to Châlons; for, in that case, surely he would have crossed at Arcis, or, if he was afraid of being anticipated there, at least at Plancy, which was nearer the main direct road. If he was going for Paris, he might do so either by Anglure and Nogent-sur-Seine, or by Sézanne and Means. Napoleon must, therefore, have advanced guards on both roads. For the former, Arrighi s division, still at Nogent, would serve; on the latter was Marmont. As for a possible move on either Châlons or Bar-sur-Aube, Ney could be sent to Arcis to look out for Blücher. Orders therefore issued at 4.30 a.m.

(1) Ney and Corbineau's Guard cavalry on Arcis.

(2) Victor and Pierre Boyer to return to Méry, seeking news of Blücher and communicating with Arrighi at Nogent and Watier's cavalry at Romilly. If Nogent was seriously threatened, Pierre Boyer was to go there and support Arrighi.

CHAPTER 6

The Second Pursuit of Blücher

Napoleon could not afford to let Blücher get a long start, if he really intended marching on Paris, an intention with which the Emperor was reluctant to credit him. He doubtless thought that Blücher would be deterred from such a march by the recollection of the disasters he had incurred when he had attempted it early in February. But it is curious how very long it took to convince Napoleon of the truth. His attitude appears to have been another example of his growing habit of regarding facts less than assumptions, and of obstinately adhering to what he had already assumed as probable, until reports finally showed that he was wrong beyond doubt.

Still, on this occasion, he recognized the possibility of Blücher's march on Paris and took precautions accordingly. It was only when these orders had issued that he directed Oudinot and Macdonald to push the army of Bohemia back to Vendœuvre and Bar-sur-Seine respectively. Macdonald was to send Jacquinot's cavalry division and Kellermann's cavalry corps to Oudinot, who would thus have two infantry corps (2nd and 7th) and the equivalent of two cavalry corps, whilst Macdonald was left with the 11th Corps and the 5th Cavalry Corps.

That evening (25th) Oudinot, now at Vendœuvre and Magny Fouchard, reported the enemy on the line Dolancourt-Spoy. Macdonald, from Bar-sur-Seine, reported 20,000 of the enemy (Bianchi, no doubt) retreating by Chaource on Tonnerre, 7000 or 8000 (3rd Corps probably) on Châtillon, and several thousand cavalry going towards Vendœuvre.

Even at 4.30 p.m., when the Emperor received Bordessoulle's and Marmont's reports of the previous day, and heard from Ney that the Arcis bridge was destroyed and hostile cavalry beyond it, he doubted as to the direction Blücher was taking. He ordered Victor to cross the Seine at Méry. Marmont at the same hour had no doubts as to Blücher; for the advance of the army of Silesia had compelled him to retire to La Ferté-Gaucher, whence he wrote to Mortier, begging him to bring his force to La Ferté-sous-Jouarre. When the two marshals could unite there next day, they would only have about 10,000 men, a force quite incapable of even seriously delaying Blücher. Bordessoulle had found himself barred from joining Marmont by a strong screen of cavalry.

At 4.30 a.m. on the 26th, Napoleon sent Pierre Boyer to join Ney, and ordered Victor to hold fast at Méry. Soon after noon he received reports of the 25th from Marmont and Bordessoulle; but even then he did not feel sure about Blücher; for, at 2.30 p.m., he wrote to Ney that the Prussian was said to be still about Baudemont. He ordered Ney to cross at Arcis, to look for Blücher, and fall on his rear. He had also ordered up Roussel d'Urbal's cavalry, from near Troyes, to join Ney. That marshal, meanwhile, crossed when he had repaired the Arcis bridge, and sent reconnaissances in all directions, as soon as he was reinforced by P. Boyer and Roussel d'Urbal.

Napoleon had, in the morning, sent orders to Oudinot to follow Schwarzenberg on Bar-sur-Aube, and to Macdonald to push on to Châtillon. Oudinot, during the day, forced the bridge at Dolancourt, and, moving up the right bank of the Aube, drove the allies from Bar-sur-Aube. For the night he took up a very faulty position on both sides of the Aube which we will describe later, when we return to Oudinot whom we shall now leave.

Macdonald got as far as Mussy-sur-Seine.

By 5 p.m. on this day (26th) Napoleon had come to the conclusion that Blücher was moving on Suzanne at any rate. Ney was told to threaten Blüchers bridges on the lower Aube, if they were still in place. If they were gone, Ney would press on Blücher's rear to relieve Marmont. Arrighi and Bordessoulle were to co-operate with Ney on the right bank of the Seine. Blücher was on no account to be allowed to establish himself at Sézanne. At 8 p.m. Marmont was ordered to unite with Mortier, and told that Arrighi and Bordessoulle would support him "when he attacked the enemy." [1]

Napoleon still scarcely believed in Blücher's march on Paris; for he tells Ney that it is "quite evident that when Blücher has no longer any bridges on the Aube, and sees a corps between him and Vitry, he will abandon all his operations, if indeed he has any beyond regaining Châlons." His orders aimed at the envelopment of Blücher by Marmont and Mortier on the west, by Arrighi and Bordessoulle on the south, and by Victor and Ney on the east. Nevertheless, Blücher's march on Paris was already in full swing. He had forced Marmont to retreat on Mortier at La Ferté-sous-Jouarre, and had his own troops spread over the country between that place and Sézanne. Marmont had sent on Ricard's division to hold the bridge at Trilport, by which he and Mortier proposed to reach Meaux next day.

When the Emperor got up at 2.30 a.m. on the 27th to issue his orders for the day, he was still in the dark as regards Blücher. "Everything," he wrote to Berthier at 3.30, "leads me to believe that Blücher has already removed his bridges on the Aube and is making for Sézanne, so as to get astride of the Vitry road." Ney and Victor, the latter crossing at Plancy, were to follow Blücher in right flank and rear, Arrighi and Bordessoulle against his left flank by Villenauxe.

At last, at 7 a.m., Marmont's report, dated thirteen hours earlier, removed all doubt as to Blücher's real direction. There was not a moment to be lost, for the army of Silesia had already gained three days' start, and the two marshals could not be expected to delay it much.

Ney, with Arrighi and Bordessoulle also under him, was to follow Blücher towards Sézanne. Marmont was informed *via*

1. For these orders see correspondence of the day.

Meaux, and it was to be bruited about so as to reach Blücher's ears, that the Emperor was in hot pursuit with the whole of the Guard. Napoleon said that he hoped to be across the Vitry road on the 28th, to dispose of the army of Silesia in three days, and then to return against that of Bohemia.

Arrighi and Bordessoulle were to march on Villenauxe, unless they found Blücher's bridges still standing and the enemy in force on the lower Aube, in which case they would move up the river to meet Victor and Ney. Napoleon still seemed to have some hope that he might find Blücher lingering on the Aube.

Troyes was now left to the care of Sebastiani with an infantry brigade, and 500 cavalry to be sent back by Macdonald. The whole of the Guard was started for Arcis.

These orders being issued, others were required for the force left behind to contain Schwarzenberg. The command of the whole was given to Macdonald, thus avoiding a repetition of the mistake of the beginning of February in leaving several independent commanders.

Macdonald was to take up a good position behind the Aube, holding Bar-sur-Aube with a strong rearguard. He was to be prepared to blow up the Dolancourt bridge, but to avoid doing so till the last moment, so as not to reveal the fact of the Emperor's departure. Everything was to be done to make Schwarzenberg believe Napoleon was still facing him. Quarters for the Emperor were to be prepared at Bar; the troops were to shout "*Vive l'Empereur*"; even Caulaincourt was to say his master was at Bar, and to send his couriers through that place. Napoleon was fully aware of the terrorizing effect of his own presence. He had recently said, "I have 50,000 men and myself; that makes 150,000."[2]

The Emperor's army was now generally disposed thus:

(1) Containing Schwarzenberg. Macdonald and Oudinot

---

2. Houssaye (p. 115) quotes Danilewski's report of Napoleon's conversation with Poltoratzki after Champaubert as containing these words. He gives the reference to *Danilewski* 1. 102; but the author has been unable to find the remark in either the English or the German translation.

with the 2nd, 7th and 11th Corps, and the 2nd, 5th and 6th Cavalry Corps, besides Allix's detachment—about 42,000 in all.

(2) Marmont and Mortier towards Meaux, about 10,000 men.

(3) Marching against Blücher's rear from Nogent, Troyes, Arcis, and Plancy under the Emperor's personal command— about 35,000 men. By evening on the 27th Napoleon had about 30,000 men collected in the area Gourganson, Sémoine, Salon, Herbisse, with cavalry at Pleurs and Œuvy. Headquarters Herbisse.

Arrighi and Bordessoulle were about Villenauxe. The latter had attempted to advance, but had to desist in face of Blücher's superior cavalry.

Napoleon's projects for the 28th are stated in a letter to Joseph. [3] Sleeping at Herbisse, he would be at Fere-Champenoise by 9 a.m. Thence, according to circumstances, he would march on Sézanne and La Ferté-Gaucher, where he would be close on Blücher's rear. Marmont and Mortier were to be ordered to press Blücher, so as to prevent that general from sending his whole force against Napoleon.

The two marshals started on the morning of the 27th from La Ferté-sous-Jouarre, after destroying the bridge there. They got across the Marne at Trilport, where Mortier turned towards Vareddes whilst Marmont marched on Meaux. He arrived there just as the garrison of National Guards had surrendered to some of Sacken's cavalry who had crossed there. Marmont quickly drove the Russians back over the Marne and blew up the bridge. Sacken also attacked the rearguard at Trilport, but, being repulsed by Ricard and Doumerc's cavalry, he fell back towards La Ferté-sous-Jouarre. The Trilport Bridge was also destroyed when Ricard had passed.

That night Mortier stood with his left at Vareddes and his right towards Meaux, where Marmont took up the defence of the Marne. Vincent, who held Château-Thierry with a small

---

3. *Corr.* 21,398, dated 5 p.m., 27th January.

detachment, was called in by Mortier. Finding the enemy on the road to La Ferté-sous-Jouarre, he made for Lizy-sur-Ourcq, where he was driven across the Ourcq and joined Mortier's left.

Blücher, meanwhile, had reached La Ferté-sous-Jouarre, had thrown two pontoon bridges at Sameron, and by evening had Kleist's corps on the right bank of the Marne. Katzeler, with the advanced guard, had seized Lizy, after driving Vincent from it. The rest of the army was still on the left bank of the Marne. At 10 a.m. on the 28th, Blücher had not realized the approach of Napoleon; for he began a letter to Schwarzenberg by saying, "It appears that up to now the Emperor Napoleon has hardly sent any detachment back against me."

Early that morning Napoleon, finding that there was only some cavalry in Fère Champenoise, left that place to be cleared by his advanced guard at Œuvy, whilst the mass of his army pushed direct on La Ferté-Gaucher. There was no fighting, except at Fère Champenoise, and in the evening Victor, the Guard, and headquarters were at Sézanne. Ney with three infantry- divisions, the Guard cavalry, and that of Roussel d'Urbal, Watier, and Sparre,[4] was at Esternay, with Arrighi and Bordessoulle close up on his left rear.

Napoleon wrote to Marmont and Mortier [5] that, if the enemy was still at La Ferté-sous-Jouarre next day, he would attack, looking to the marshals to support him from the opposite direction.

Blücher had now open to him four courses:

(1) He might push forward on Meaux and Paris which was the course he said, in his letter of 10 a.m. on the 28th, he meant to follow.

(2) He might get away northwards on the right bank of the Marne towards Soissons, so as to join Bülow from Laon and Winzingerode from Reims, trusting to the protection of his rear

---

4. Sparre's brigade of 1000 cavalry had just arrived from Soult's army.
5. He had to send orders *via* Paris as he had no direct communication.

by the Marne with its broken bridges.

(3) He might continue on Paris by Lizy, turning the marshals' left and still protected by the Marne.

(4) He might, when he realized that Napoleon was in his rear, face about for a battle with the Emperor, as the latter expected.

On the whole, the second course was the wisest, though to a man of Blücher's temperament there was a strong temptation to continue on Paris, or to fight Napoleon.

Before Blücher had finished his letter of 10 a.m. he received one, dated 25th February, from Schwarzenberg, saying that the army of Bohemia would continue its retreat until Blücher's pressure on Napoleon's communications allowed resumption of the offensive. For the present, the parts played by Schwarzenberg and Blücher in August, 1813, were to be reversed, Blücher now acting on the offensive, Schwarzenberg on the defensive. To Blücher command was now given over the corps of Winzingerode, Bulow, and the Duke of Weimar. Holland and Belgium, occupied by Bernadotte, would now form a new base for Blücher's operations. In conclusion, he was requested to establish a flying post of Cossacks between the two armies.

Blücher now finished his letter, saying the flying post was not possible, but he would keep Winzingerode at Reims as a link between them, whilst he would order Bulow to advance on Paris by Soissons and Dommartin, so as to be able to unite with him for a battle if the Emperor followed him. Winzingerode had been asked by Blücher on the 26th to come to Meaux; but, fearing Mortier on his flank at Villers-Cotterets, the Russian had only sent Tettenborn through Epernay. Blücher now ordered Winzingerode to stop at Reims. To the Duke of Weimar he wrote to wait till Bernadotte's Swedes could take over the blockade of the Netherland fortresses, but to place himself ready to move south if required.

Langeron's command, which also belonged to the Silesian army, was much dispersed. Nine thousand were before Mayence; Kapzewitch, the remains of Olsufiew's corps, and Korff's cavalry were with Blücher; St. Priest's corps was at St. Dizier. Langeron himself had started to join Blücher on the Aube with a regiment of cavalry and one of Cossacks. Finding the Prussian general gone, he went to Vertus. There he met Tettenborn, who told him Napoleon was at Fère-Champenoise. Thence he went to Epernay where he joined Colonel von Lobenthal, who was in command of some 2000 reinforcements for Blücher.

The most important fighting on the 28th had been with the two marshals. They had inferred, from Sacken's retreat on the 27th, that Blücher was going to turn them by Lizy-sur-Ourcq, and decided that their own best course was to move up the Marne towards Lizy, where they knew Kleist had been the evening before. Kleist, though he had no supports at hand, repaired the Lizy bridge and moved down the right bank of the Ourcq and Marne to take post behind the Therouanne. Thence he was driven back up the river, destroying again the Lizy bridge as he passed, till at midnight he stood (still on the right bank) behind the Gergogne brook. Marmont was in front of him at May-en-Multien, Mortier at Lizy, where he repulsed two of Kapzewitch's regiments sent to support Kleist. Sacken had also marched to the sound of the guns in that direction. Kleist had lost 1000 men and believed, from the shouts of "*Vive l'Empereur*," that he was opposed to Napoleon.

On the 1st March Blücher still had only rather vague reports of the French advance on his rear. He had heard from Korff that the enemy was at Suzanne, but knew nothing of his strength, or whether Napoleon was present. Nevertheless, remembering the events of the middle of February, he thought it safer to get behind the Marne. For a moment he was inclined to meet the new enemy with Sacken, Kapzewitch, and Yorck, leaving Kleist to deal with the marshals; but Kleist had been doing badly; therefore, Kapzewitch and Korff were ordered to march on Gesvres; Yorck to Crouy, his march being covered by Sacken at Lizy.

Kleist was to make a fresh advance on Meaux; all baggage and pontoons to move to Gandelu on the road to Oulchy. Blücher proposed to fall back on Oulchy in order to gather in Bülow and Winzingerode. The country he would have to pass through on the left bank of the Ourcq was marshy, with bad roads rendered still worse by the thaw which had now succeeded the frost of the last few days.

By 2 p.m., when Napoleon's horse artillery at La Ferté-sous-Jouarre was firing at the enemy across the river, all the allied troops were across, and the bridges removed or destroyed. That night the Emperor had cavalry in La Ferté-sous-Jouarre, Ney and Arrighi three or four miles behind it, the Guard at Rebais, Victor at La Ferté-Gaucher. Bordessoulle was at Coulommiers, on his way to join the marshals. Napoleon was hung up by the impossibility of crossing at La Ferté-sous-Jouarre; for the permanent bridge was badly damaged, and he had no pontoons, a fact of which he was constantly complaining to Paris. Whoever was in fault, he had undoubtedly been seriously hampered by it, both at Nogent on the 19th and here. Marmont reported the enemy was marching on La Ferté-Milon by both banks of the Ourcq.

The Emperor's plan of crushing Blücher against the Marne, between his own army and that of the marshals, had failed. He saw that the repair of the bridge at La Ferté-sous-Jouarre would delay him, and, to add to his troubles, he heard that Oudinot had been badly beaten at Bar-sur-Aube on the 27th February. He could only rely on Schwarzenberg's notorious slowness and irresolution to prevent him pushing his way to Paris. The Emperor now contemplated a new scheme. He proposed to drive Blücher far away northwards, and then to march by Châlons, calling up the weakly blockaded garrisons of his fortresses in Lorraine. Reinforced by them, he would march on Schwarzenberg's communications, a move which, looking to the Austrian's excessive sensitiveness on this point, might be expected to bring him back, even if he were already at the gates of the capital.

During this 1st March Kleist's fresh advance towards Meaux had been repulsed, and Marmont and Mortier occupied at night practically the same positions as in the previous night. When, at 5 p.m. on the 2nd, Napoleon heard of this, he replied to

Mortier that his own force would be ready to cross the Marne in a couple of hours. He supposed Blücher was retreating on La Ferté-Milon, and that the two marshals had between them nearly 25,000 men and 80 guns. [6] He added, "As soon as I am reassured as to the offensive movement against you, my intention is to move on my fortresses, marching in the direction of Châlons (for they are not really blockading any of the places; so that the garrison of Metz makes sorties nearly to Nancy), and all these reinforcements would largely increase my army." [7]

The Emperor was again suffering from excessive optimism; for it was not for another sixteen hours that the bridge was ready. It was only in the morning of the 2nd March that Blücher heard positively from Tettenborn that he had Napoleon in person following him. His troops were undoubtedly suffering very severely in the marshy country, cut off from their old line of communications, and with the new one not yet in working order. Russians and Prussians vied with one another in pillaging and burning, in a way which horrified so stern a disciplinarian as Yorck. [8]

Müffling describes their appearance two days later at Soissons. "Our men looked remarkable with their faces blackened by bivouac smoke, and long strangers to the luxury of a razor, but with an expression of energy and bodily strength—with tattered cloaks, badly patched trousers, and unpolished arms—the cavalry on their ill-cleaned, but neighing horses—all with a true martial bearing." [9] They were far from being the demoralized crew that Napoleon described on the 1st March. [10] So satisfied was Napoleon on that date that he would soon dispose of the army of Silesia, that he told Caulaincourt (who had just written

---

6. They had little more than two-thirds of that number, though Mortier had been reinforced by Poret de Morvan's provisional Young Guard division (4800), and Marmont by 1100 cavalry and 48 guns from Paris, and there were 600 Polish lancers and another battalion on the way, as well as Bordessoulle's 800 cavalry.
7. *Corr.* 21,416.
8. Droysen, *Life of Yorck*, 3. 332.
9. *Passages from my Life*, p. 148.
10. *Corr.* 21,418.

that the allies would consider the negotiations at an end, unless their new terms were accepted by the 10th March) that nothing would induce him to accept less than the Frankfort terms.

During the 2nd, Blücher moved but little. He knew not the whereabouts of Bülow and Winzingerode. A message to him had been intercepted which would have told him that Winzingerode was due at Fismes on the 1st, whence he would march on Soissons, under an arrangement with Bülow to try a combined coup de main against the place. Blücher now imposed another night march on his weary troops. They were to take position on the north bank of the Ourcq, where it flows from east to west before turning south about La Ferté-Milon. Blücher was at Oulchy-le-Château at midnight on the 2nd, whence he wrote to Bülow that he must now abandon his advance on Paris, and concentrate with the army of Silesia about Oulchy for a battle with Napoleon.

He also called up Winzingerode to between Fismes and Soissons for the same purpose. Further, he made inquiries as to what bridges were available on the Aisne near Soissons. It was only when these letters had gone that he heard of Bülow's and Winzingerode's combined movement on Soissons. A letter from Winzingerode, dated Soissons, 3rd March, 5 a.m., informed Blücher that an attempt on Soissons on the previous evening had failed, that Winzingerode was sending the greater part of his infantry across the Aisne at Vailly to join Bülow, that, with one brigade, he would remain before Soissons during the 3rd, and then, unless circumstances changed, he would make for Fismes.

At 7 a.m. Winzingerode replied to Blücher's last orders, saying there was no good position for defence against an attack from Soissons or Villers-Cotterets. He would await further orders to march to Oulchy or elsewhere. Before this letter reached him, Blücher had decided to join Billow and Winzingerode beyond the Aisne. All his baggage was sent off to Fismes at noon, the pontoons were sent to Buzancy, and Winzingerode was asked to find a good place for the passage, and to mask Soissons. If possible, Blücher wished to cross at Venizel. The army was ordered to march by Buzancy to the Aisne above Soissons.

With the French there was no serious contact, except in the direction of Marmont and Mortier, who had some fighting with Kleist about Neuilly-St. Front, as they pursued him towards Oulchy.

Napoleon, only able to commence passing the Marne at 10 a.m., had his army by evening of the 3rd in the following positions:

(1) Marmont, Mortier and Bordessoulle between Neuilly-St. Front and the Ourcq.

(2) Grouchy's cavalry at La Croix, in touch with them.

(3) Nansouty about Rocourt, with a detachment at Fère-en-Tardenois.

(4) Headquarters, Ney (with the divisions Pierre Boyer and Meunier) and the Guard at Bézu-St. Germain.

(5) Victor approaching Château-Thierry from La Ferté-Gaucher direct, and Curial's division (of Ney's corps) waiting for him at the former.

(6) Arrighi halted at Montreuil-aux-Lions on account of the exhaustion of his young troops.

Blücher, meanwhile, on reaching Buzancy had found his task much facilitated by news that Soissons had capitulated, and would be evacuated at 4 p.m.

The surrender of Soissons has been the subject of much controversy, and a small volume could be filled by a discussion of its effect on the campaign. Thiers, Houssaye, and other French writers agree with Napoleon in saying it saved Blücher from annihilation. The same is said by the partisans of Bülow and Winzingerode. Müffling, Clausewitz, and most German writers say that Blücher could, as he proposed, have got across the Aisne above Soissons in ample time.

It is impossible, in this work, to go in detail into the controversy, but we shall state the general conclusions we draw from it. Naturally, Blücher now decided to use the stone bridge at Soissons, as well as his own pontoon bridges. He was able to begin his passage in the afternoon of the 3rd, and to complete it in the evening of the 4th.

One conclusion we may state at once, namely, that there is little or nothing to be said for Moreau, the French commandant of Soissons. He had a small but veteran garrison, [11] the fortifications were certainly useless against a regular siege, but still sufficient to have enabled him to hold out for twenty-four or thirty-six hours against almost any force; he actually repulsed, without difficulty, Winzingerode's attack in the evening of the 2nd. Yet, during the succeeding night he allowed himself to be cajoled, threatened, and flattered into a dereliction of his obvious duty by surrendering the place without another fight, on condition that the garrison should march out, in the direction of Compiègne, with six guns and the honours of war.

He did not even blow up the bridge before capitulating. The terms offered him should have sufficed to show him what importance the allies attached to the place, and how very uncertain they felt of being able to storm it. Marmont spoke none too strongly when he wrote to Berthier that this was an excellent opportunity for hanging a commandant of a fortress." Nor was Napoleon unjustified in saying, "It was not for General Moreau to reason; since he had been ordered to hold Soissons, he should have held it.

Soissons was evidently not a fortress, but only a military post guarding the Aisne bridge, where he ought to hold out to the last extremity, as a defile is held till one is wiped out." [12]That incontrovertible statement overthrows the one possible excuse which might have been put forward, namely, that Moreau was ignorant of the approach of Napoleon. Marmont and Mortier heard of the surrender of Soissons at Hartennes in the morning of the 4th; yet the Emperor was not informed till late in the

---

11. Chiefly the "Regiment of the Vistula."

12. *Corr.* 21,451. Napoleon, in his usual form, ordered Moreau to be tried and publicly shot in Paris, but, before the formal trial could be completed, the Emperor had fallen and Moreau escaped punishment.

night of the 4th-5th. The marshals, instead of pushing on with all their force, and trying to hamper Blücher's passage of the Aisne, only sent on their cavalry which could do nothing but idly watch the passage from afar.

Blücher crossed by the stone bridge and by three pontoon bridges. It took him twenty-four hours or more. If he had not had Soissons, he would still have had his pontoon bridges, and a bridge (not passable for wheeled traffic) at Vailly. Under these circumstances, the passage would have required longer, but, on the other hand, he might have hurried up under the pressure of need. He was certainly saved a good deal of annoyance and some delay by the marshals' inaction, but they could not have delayed him very long. Even without the Soissons Bridge, he would certainly have been over by the morning of the 5th.

Could Napoleon have stopped him if Soissons had held out?

To answer the question we must examine the Emperor's views and movements on the 4th when, as we know, he still believed Soissons to be holding out. Marmont had judged rightly that Blücher was making for Soissons, but Napoleon persisted in believing he was trying to escape, between the Aisne and the Vesle, to Reims. He had clearly no idea that Blücher was changing his line of communications from Châlons to Laon. He knew nothing of Bülow's having even reached Laon. Had he believed Blücher to be making for the Aisne at or a little above Soissons, he would naturally have pursued him direct, in the hope of driving him against the river before he could be ready to pass.

But, with the belief he held, his movements were directed to intercept Blücher's eastward march about Fismes. On the evening of the 4th he was at Fismes with the Old Guard, Nansouty, and Ney's two divisions, and had cavalry posts watching the Aisne at Pont Arcy, Maizy, and Roucy. Grouchy's cavalry was astride of the Vesle in the space Paars, Bazoche, Mont Notre Dame. Victor and Curial's division were at Fère-en-Tardenois, and Arrighi at Château-Thierry. Laferrière's Guard cavalry division was on the march to Reims.

At this moment Blücher was completing his passage of the Aisne. He had cavalry posts along the right bank of the Aisne all the way to Berry-au-Bac; his baggage was on the way to Berry-au-Bac, part of it had been taken at Courcelles, but recaptured by Blücher's cavalry, which extended up both banks of the Vesle as far as the line Limé-Courcelles. Napoleon expected to find Blücher at Fismes, though he admitted the possibility that he might be trying to reach Laon by crossing near Soissons and masking that place. In that case, if the Emperor crossed the Aisne north of Fismes, he might still reach Laon first.

These being Napoleon's views, he had nothing nearer to Blücher than Grouchy's cavalry, which was opposed by Blücher's. The nearest French infantry of the Emperor's own force was at Fismes, some seventeen miles from Soissons, and about ten from the Vailly footbridge. Under these circumstances, how is it possible to believe that Napoleon could have cut off any large portion of Blücher's army south of the Aisne by the morning of the 5th, the latest time at which the allies would have been crossing, even if they had not had the Soissons bridge? Our conclusion, therefore, must be contrary to that which represents Blücher as saved solely by the capture of Soissons. At the same time, the possession of that bridge certainly saved him some anxiety.

Even at 2 p.m. on the 4th, Napoleon knew nothing of Bülow; for at that hour Berthier wrote to Marmont: "The Emperor thinks you ought to have news of Bülow, who is believed to be towards Avesnes." [13] He did know that Winzingerode had joined Blücher, and that the two together must have 70,000 men. Yet, though he had only 48,000 men, including those of the two marshals, he proposed a concentric movement with two separate bodies; for he wrote to Marmont: "If the enemy has marched on Soissons, it is probably in order to reach Laon, and, if you are at Soissons with the Duke of Treviso, we can, on our side, arrive at the same time as you at Laon."

There is some difficulty in arriving at the numbers on either

13. Avesnes to Soissons is at least three marches.

side, mainly caused by Houssaye's attempt to show that the allied numbers were less than generally represented by their own authorities. At p. 200, n. 1, of *1814*, he tries to show that Blücher had only 84,000 men on the 10th at Laon, which, allowing for intermediate losses, would mean about 90,000 on the 4th March.

On the other hand *Weil* (3. 71), a very careful and accurate French authority, puts the number at nearly 113,000. *Plotho* (3. 293) says Blücher had 110,000 at Laon, say 115,000 on the 4th March. *Janson* (2. 101) follows Weil. Müffling (*Passages, etc.*, 151) says "over 100,000," and that he took the numbers from the daily states. Again (p. 473) he says 109,000. Droysen (*Life of Yorck*, 2. 331) gives details: Langeron 26,000; Sacken 13,700; Winzingerode 30,000; Bülow 16,900; Yorck 13,500; Kleist 10,600; total 110,700.

Bogdanowitch (1. 308) says 105,000. Damitz's figures are a confusion of Bogdanowitch's and of little value. On the whole, the weight of evidence seems to be in favour of 110,000 or more. As for Napoleon, Houssaye (p. 200, n. 1) says he had scarcely 35,000 at Laon, including Marmont and Mortier, say 42,000 on the 4th March.

This seems incomprehensible; for (p. 127, n. 2) he gives Napoleon alone, without the marshals, 34,233 on the 2nd March, and apparently omits Bordessoulle's 800 cavalry sent to the marshals. He puts Marmont and Mortier at 10,502 (p. 124, n. 4), on the 26th February, but to that total have to be added the reinforcements from Paris (Poret de Morvau, etc.) received in the beginning of March amounting to 6055 (p. 126, n. 2). (He forgets the 600 Polish lancers and a battalion following next day.)

Thus we may say that on the 28th February Napoleon had about 35,000 men besides 17,000 with the marshals. The Emperor had practically no fighting up to the 4th March, and we may accept Houssaye's figure for him of 34,233 on that date. Of their 17,000 Marmont and Mortier cannot have lost more than 3,000 in their various combats with Kleist. The total French forces on the 4th March may, therefore, be taken as at least 48,000.

Knowing Blücher had been joined by Winzingerode, but not that he had got Billow's 17,000 also, he should have put Blücher's force at about 90,000, though he probably thought it less. Anyhow, if he took Blücher as having only 70,000, he was opposed with 48,000 to 70,000. As a matter of fact he had about 110,000 against him.

CHAPTER 7

Craonne

Napoleon's first idea on the 5th March was to cross the Aisne due north of Fismes and move on Laon, thereby inducing Blücher also to make for Laon from Soissons. But he abandoned the idea because, having no pontoons, he would have to rely on trestle bridges, and because he found Blücher extended much farther east than he had believed. Moreover, Marmont reported that Blücher was already retreating on Laon.

The Emperor, therefore, decided to cross at Berry-au-Bac, where there was a new stone bridge, and to march on Laon by the road from Reims, At 10 a.m. he heard that Corbineau, whom he had sent to Reims on the previous day with Laferrière's Guard cavalry division, had taken the place.

Everything under the Emperor's immediate command was ordered on Berry-au-Bac. Mortier, who had been ordered to Braisne, was now to continue on Berry-au-Bac. Marmont was to reach Braisne in the night of the 5th-6th. By that time Napoleon would be sure that Blücher was not going to try a move on Paris by the Soissons road. During this day Marmont and Mortier tried a *coup de main* against Soissons, but were beaten off by the strong garrison which Blücher had left there, with a loss of 1500 men. Consequently, even Mortier did not start for Braisne till 9 p.m.

When Napoleon reached Berry-au-Bac, at 4 p.m., he found that Nansouty and Pac had driven Russian cavalry from it back beyond Corbény. Russian infantry were reported about

Craonelle. Ney (divisions Pierre Boyer [1] and Meunier) joined Nansouty at Corbény in the evening. The Old Guard was with the Emperor about Berry-au-Bac and La Ville aux Bois. Victor's corps and Curial's division stretched from Fismes towards Berry-au-Bac. Arrighi was at Fère-en-Tardenois. Marmont and Mortier were only about to march from in front of Soissons. Roussel d'Urbal's dragoons were waiting to be relieved by Mortier at Braisne.

As for Blücher, the main part of his army was behind the Aisne north of Soissons, but he had detachments watching the river eastwards up to Craonelle, Craonne, and on the Reims-Laon road in front of Corbény. He also still had cavalry on the lower Vesle. It had been driven from Braisne by Roussel d'Urbal. The eastward force towards Craonne was part of Winzingerode's corps which had moved there in consequence of news of the French passage at Berry-au-Bac.

Blücher during the day had come to the conclusion that Napoleon was marching on Laon by the Reims road. His first orders for the 6th were to the following effect:—

(1) Baggage to move to behind Laon.

(2) Winzingerode to watch the enemy from between Braye and Cerny.

(3) Sacken to hold Vailly, and take post between Ostel and Braye.

(4) Langeron, leaving 5000 men in Soissons, to fall back on Aizy with the rest, watching the Aisne from Celles to Soissons.

(5) Kleist to stand between Filain and La Royère.

(6) Yorck between Jouy and Pargny.

(7) Bülow to fall back towards Laon by the Soissons road.

Napoleon had, on the 5th, sent orders to Janssens at Mézières to fall, with the garrisons of the Ardennes fortresses, on

---

1. Pierre Boyer's command consisted of one brigade only (about 1900 men), the other was with Macdonald.

Blücher's rear at Laon. Durutte, at Metz, was to break out with all his forces, and to collect the garrisons of the neighbouring fortresses. On the 6th the Emperor announced to Joseph his intention, after pushing Blücher on Laon, of marching against Schwarzenberg by Châlons or Arcis-sur-Aube.

By noon on that day he had 30,500 men about Corbény, La Ville aux Bois, and Berry-au-Bac. He proposed to send an advanced guard consisting of Nansouty, Ney, Friant's Old Guard, and the reserve artillery on Laon by Festieux. Victor would remain on the watch about Craonne and Pontavert. But, before advancing definitely on Laon, it was necessary to be sure that Blücher was not hanging back on the heights of the right bank of the Aisne.

Here it will be convenient to describe the country in the triangle Soissons, Laon, Berry-au-Bac which was to form the theatre of operations during the next few days. [2]

The so-called Chemin des Dames, starting from a point on the Soissons-Laon road near the inn of L'Ange Gardien, runs eastward along a continuous ridge to Craonne near the eastern end of the ridge. Just west of that village it descends along the southern face to Chevreux, and rises again slightly to join the Reims-Laon road at Corbény. The ridge averages an elevation of some 400 feet above the valley of the Aisne. It varies much in width, from a couple of hundred yards or less, where valleys from the north and south nearly meet, to two miles or more along the spurs on either side. The spurs on the north side are generally shorter than on the south, and the slope is steeper to the valley of the Lette, or Ailette, a stream which runs generally parallel to that of the Aisne to join the Oise. The slopes on this side are much wooded, and the valley is marshy.

North of the Lette are more hills of about the same elevation as those on the south, but forming a less distinct ridge. These northern heights again fall to a wooded marshy plain extend-

---

2. The author had the advantage in September, 1912, of going over a great part of this country with the French 4th division (2nd corps) which manoeuvred on general ideas based on those of Napoleon of 1814.

ing over some four miles up to Laon. West of the Soissons–Laon road is a hilly country, the eastern border of which is within two or three miles of Laon. North of Laon, and east of the Reims–Laon road, the country is practically level.

Laon itself stands on an isolated hill rising some 350 feet above the plain. Viewed from the plain on the north, it reminds those who have seen Gwalior of that Indian rock fortress. The town occupies the summit, and even now there remains much of the old walls which once made it a very strong fortress. At the foot of the hill are several suburbs, of which the most important for our purpose are Semilly at the south-west corner, and Ardon to the south, the latter traversed by a marshy brook of the same name which flows to join the Lette beyond the road to Soissons some five or six miles south-west of Laon. The Soissons–Laon road runs through or over hills till it reaches the plain south of Laon. The Reims–Laon road runs mostly outside the hills which only cross it with outlying spurs for a mile or two on either side of Festieux. The chief distances, as the crow flies, are: Soissons to Laon eighteen miles; Soissons to Berry-au-Bac twenty-six miles; Berry-au-Bac to Laon eighteen miles.

The plain south of Laon, between the Reims and Soissons roads, is extremely difficult for transverse communication, owing to the marshy fields in which, though the ground looks solid enough at a distance, a horse will sink to its hocks. The villages in the neighbourhood are generally very defensible. Some of them, Bruyères for instance, are old fortified villages with some of the walls still standing.

As Pierre Boyer marched on Laon on the morning of the 6th, he encountered little or no resistance up to Maison Rouge, and the Polish lancers reached Festieux. On the left it was different. Meunier found Russians holding the Abbey of Vauclerc; two battalions of Old Guard under Caramon had to drive the enemy from Chevreux and Craonne, and found themselves unable to take the little plateau above these villages. This little plateau must be cleared, so the Emperor ordered Meunier to co-operate, by Vauclerc and Heurtebise, with the attack from the south. He took the Abbey at 5 p.m., and then engaged in a desperate fight for Heurtebise, the farm which stands on the narrow neck between the little plateau and the greater farther west. The farm, taken and retaken several times, remained in possession of the Russians, but they withdrew from the little plateau, which was occupied by Caramon facing Heurtebise.

Meunier spent the night in the valley north of Heurtebise. Boyer was at Bouconville, whither he had been sent to support Meunier. Of the Old Guard one brigade was at Chevreux and Craonne, the other at Corbény. On the left was Exelmans' cavalry at Craonelle and Ouiches. Boyer de Rebeval's division was at La Ville-aux-Bois. Charpentier, Curial, and the cavalry of Roussel d'Urbal, Colbert, and Laferrière were at Berry-au-Bac. Only Mortier at Cormicy, Arrighi at Roucy, and Marmont at Braisne were still south of the Aisne. When Blücher issued his first orders, given above, for the 6th, he had not heard of Winzingerode's eastward movement on the 5th.

By 2 p.m. he was satisfied that Napoleon was making, not a tactical turning movement to be combined with a frontal attack from the Aisne, but a strategical turning movement by the Reims road with his whole army. He therefore issued a general order for the movement of the Silesian army along the great ridge, hoping to fall upon the Emperor's left flank as he was spread out in the march from Berry-au-Bac to Laon. Blücher rode over to Heurtebise, where he arrived just as Meunier's last attack had been repulsed.

He now saw that he must expect to be attacked next day from the east along the Chemin des Dames. Napoleon had equally come to the conclusion that he could not venture on the march to Laon without first brushing aside the force which stood on his left flank, and which was estimated at 20,000 men. Blücher now took up a new scheme. Woronzow, with the whole of Winzingerode's infantry and part of his cavalry, would meet Napoleon's attack. Sacken would stand as his support about Froidmont, with his cavalry in front.

Whilst Woronzow held Napoleon in front, Winzingerode

with 10,000 or 12,000 cavalry [3] would move by the north side of the Lette valley on Festieux, whence he would descend on Napoleon's right flank and rear as the Emperor attacked Woronzow from the east. All this cavalry was to be first assembled at Filain, and then to march so as to be at Festieux by daybreak. But Winzingerode had his own cavalry towards Craonne, and he would have to make a march of several miles before he even joined the rest of his force at Filain. The effect of this we shall see later.

Winzingerode was to be followed by the infantry of Yorck, Kleist, and Langeron [4] to support his attack on Napoleon's right and rear. Bülow would march on Laon.

Napoleon, who knew nothing of Blüchers movements or intentions, heard that an old fellow-student at Brienne, M. de Bussy, was now mayor of Beaurieux. Sending for him he obtained a great deal of information as to the locality, to which he listened attentively, and according to which he arranged his plan of battle.

His orders of 4 a.m. on the 7th contemplated a frontal attack on the plateau west of the neck of Heurtebise with Victor and Curial, supported if necessary by Friant and the reserve artillery.

The enemy's left flank would be attacked at Ailles and to the south-east of it by Pierre Boyer and Meunier, whilst his right would be turned by Nansouty with Exelmans' cavalry by the heights of Vassogne.

The rest of the army between Berry-au-Bac and Corbény would be ready to move as might be required. Marmont, who was farthest behind, was to rejoin the army at once, and, if it should prove feasible to cross the Aisne about Maizy, he might be able to save some hours by doing so.

By 8 a.m. on the 7th Napoleon, as the result of reports and of a personal reconnaissance from the plateau north of Oulches, was satisfied that Woronzow meant to fight. He was drawn up

---

3. 5500 of his own, all Langeron's cavalry and Yorck's reserve cavalry.
4. One of Langeron's brigades was still to remain in Soissons.

across the Chemin des Dames, with his front line just west of the woods Marion and Quatre Heures [5] some 1100 yards west of Heurtebise which was still occupied. The second and third lines were at intervals of 400 or 500 yards. The left rested on the village of Ailles down the slope of the Lette valley, the right (formed by one cavalry and three Cossack regiments) stood on the heights above Vassogne, a total length of about 1½ miles.

Woronzow had ninety-six guns, of which thirty-six were opposite the gap between the two woods, sweeping the neck of Heurtebise, twelve more on the right crossed fire with these, eighteen fired on the valley of the Lette, and thirty were in reserve. Altogether he had about 16,000 infantry and 2000 cavalry. Behind him was Sacken's cavalry under Wassiltchikow about 4000 strong. Sacken's infantry at Froidmont was too far off to give prompt support.

The battle began about 9 a.m. with a cannonade by part of the French artillery from north of Oulches to which the Russians replied. The distance being too great in those days, little harm was done. The cannonade did have one unfortunate effect, in inducing the impetuous Ney to believe that it was time for him to launch his attack against the Russian left. Though he had distinct instructions to await further orders before doing so, he hurled Pierre Boyer's brigade against Ailles, and Meunier's against the heights south-east of it.

He was thus beginning a flank attack long before the frontal attack could develop and fix the enemy in that direction. Victor's men had been delayed by the state of the roads, slippery from frost. When they did begin to arrive, the first thing which had to be done was to move Boyer de Rebeval to the right to bring relief, by an attack on the Bois Marion, to Meunier, who had already lost heavily. Nansouty also had to be sent forward on the opposite flank, and more cavalry to support him was called up from Corbény. About this hour (11 a.m.) Heurtebise caught fire

---

5. These two woods were on either side of the Chemin des Dames just where the neck leading westwards from Heurtebise opens out into a broader plateau. Both seem to have been cut down.

and was evacuated by the Russians.

For Ney's early commencement Napoleon must bear some of the blame; for, as at Bautzen, he had sent Ney orders without vouchsafing an explanation of his own general plan, which would have shown Ney the necessity for waiting to advance until the frontal attack was fully developed. But Ney must bear the whole blame for sending on his infantry far in advance of his artillery, and without any preparation of the attack by artillery fire. The result was that both Meunier and Pierre Boyer suffered terrible losses from the Russian guns on the edge of the plateau, and their attacks had been repulsed, or been brought to a standstill. About 11.30 Ney's artillery, now up, caused considerable damage to the Russian left at Ailles and on the plateau, and it showed some tendency to fall back. Then Ney led Meunier's men forward in person up the steep slope at the top of which they at last arrived.

Nansouty, meanwhile, on the southern flank, had been more successful. Screening his advance with a dismounted advance guard, he had arrived on the spur between Vassogne and Paissy, and had defeated the 2000 cavalry and Cossacks on Woronzow's right, as well as two battalions sent to their support

It was about noon when Boyer de Rebeval, Victor's leading division, attacked the Bois Marion, thereby withdrawing the enemy's attention from the harassed troops of Meunier. He captured the wood but was driven back into it when he attempted to debouch.

At 1 p.m. his division and Meunier's were in imminent of being driven again from the plateau. They suffered heavily from a Russian battery on the crest south of Ailles, which village still remained untaken by Pierre Boyer. Momentary relief was afforded by a charge of Sparre's dragoons against this battery, in which both Sparre and Grouchy were wounded. Then the Russians drove Meunier's and Rebeval's troops back. The former fled down the hill, but Rebeval's men were rallied behind the Bois Marion which they still held.

At 1.45 the 1st cavalry division of the Guard executed a desperate charge from Heurtebise against the enemy's guns across the Chemin des Dames. The guns were reached, but then the cavalry were driven back by a furious fire. They had nevertheless gained time for the arrival of Charpentier's division of Victor's corps, which advanced along the southern slopes towards the Bois de Quatre Heures. Sheltered by the slope from the Russian artillery, they took the wood with ease. By 2.30 Charpentier's left joined Nansouty's right and began to force in the right of the Russian infantry. Rebeval's guns and those of the Guard were now between the two woods. Nansouty, after driving the enemy's cavalry back to the head of the Paissy valley, had been forced by artillery fire to retire again.

Ney, meanwhile, had, at 2 p.m., once more got back to the edge of the plateau with Meunier's men.

It was about this time that Pierre Boyer reported the appearance of a hostile force towards Chamomile, on his right flank. [6]

With his right thus threatened from beyond the Lette, the Emperor saw that it was time for him to produce the "*evènement*," as he called the great final blow with which he was accustomed to complete the defeat of an enemy already almost exhausted.

At 2.30 he ordered the reserve of artillery, from in rear of Heurtebise, to join the Guard's and Victor's guns beyond the narrow neck. When this was done, Drouot poured upon the Russian centre a blast of grape from eighty-eight guns at a distance of only a few hundred yards.

At this moment, Pierre Boyer had at last taken Ailles, the garrison of which streamed up on to the plateau.

The remains of the divisions of Rebeval and Meunier were advancing from the neighbourhood of the Bois Marion, whilst Charpentier and the cavalry were pressing the Russian right.

Curial, Friant, and the 3rd division of the cavalry of the Guard then moved forward through Drouot's guns (the fire of which they temporarily masked) along the Chemin des Dames.

---

6. What they saw was Kleist marching for the turning movement in support of Winzingerode's cavalry.

The Russians now fell back in good order before this advance to a position with their right at the head of the Paissy valley, left about 800 yards S.S.W. of the church at Ailles.

The Emperor could now no longer be alarmed by the report from Ney that a hostile column was moving from Colligis to Montbérault, up the farther slope of the Lette valley. A counter-attack by a few Russian battalions was repulsed, and at 4 p.m. the enemy retired to yet another parallel position, of which the right was about Troyan.

Belliard, now commanding *vice* Grouchy wounded, succeeded in turning this from the Troyan valley, but, on the slope beyond Troyan, was charged by the whole of the Russian cavalry (that which had been on Woronzow's right and Wassiltchikow's in reserve) and driven back into the valley. The French Guard batteries were now in position along the road across the plateau from Ailles to Moulins, and Pierre Boyer was coming up from Ailles against the Russian left

Once more the Russians fell back, covered devotedly by their cavalry, and again took post across the plateau in front of Courtecon. Then Boyer de Rebeval and Charpentier observed infantry moving down towards the Lette which they threw into disorder with artillery fire. Its discomfiture was completed by P. Boyer, but it got away to Chevregny, in which direction it could not be followed, owing to the presence of allied troops north of the Lette at Chevregny and Trucy.

It was between 7 and 8 p.m. when the French pursuit ended. The mass of their army bivouacked in the following positions, facing towards the Lette valley into which their outposts pushed. Mortier was on the right at Malval farm with Napoleon and the Guard infantry behind him at Braye. In the centre Ney, at Froidmont, had Belliard's cavalry behind him at Ostel. On the left Charpentier's division and the Guard cavalry were about the Chemin des Dames south-west of Filain, and Colbert's cavalry division was on their left rear about Aizy. Bordessoulle was left behind, at Heurtebise, as a connecting link with the troops about Berry-au-Bac. Marmont, who had been unable to cross the Aisne at Maizy, still had a detachment at Fismes and some cavalry at Braisne, watching lest Blücher should turn back on Paris. The bulk of Marmont's troops with Arrighi's division were at Berry-au-Bac, and a detachment of Polish lancers held Corbény. The allies' outposts stretched from near l'Ange Gardien through Pargny and along the north bank of the Lette as far as the longitude of Courtecon. Behind these, Langeron and Sacken were on the roads to Laon. Yorck had got as far as Leuilly, and Bülow had already reached Laon. In another group stood Kleist and Winzingerode's cavalry about Festieux, with outposts towards Corbény.

What, meanwhile, had become of Winzingerode's turning movement? At 10 a.m. Blücher, then with Woronzow, hurried off to see after Winzingerode, who was reported to be still at Chevregny, though he should have been at Festieux by daybreak. As we have implied, Blücher's own order was largely responsible for the delay. When Winzingerode got back late at night on the 6th to Filain with his own cavalry, he found Langeron's and Yorck's cavalry in bivouac for the night, saddles off, and the men sleeping or cooking. He, therefore, deferred his start till morning, but made no attempt to reconnoitre the road by which he was to march. When he did start, he took the longer road by Chevregny, Presles, Bruyères, and Parfondru, instead of the shorter by Trucy, Colligis, and Montbérault which Kleist chose.

At 11 a.m. he and Kleist crossed one another at Chevregny, the cavalry still not clear of the marshes of the Lette. Kleist, who also started in the morning of the 7th, reached Festieux by 4 p.m. At 2 p.m. Blücher came up with Winzingerode who was even then only at Bruyères. It was far too late to hope for any success against Napoleon's flank and rear. What Blücher said at Bruyères is, perhaps fortunately for polite ears, not recorded.

The battle of Craonne was but a Pyrrhic victory for the Emperor. It had, too, entirely deranged his plan of marching on Laon by the Reims road to anticipate Blücher, or to cut off all of his army that had not passed Laon. The Emperor had had to take a position immensely strong in those days, and defended with desperate courage by Woronzow's Russians who numbered, including Wassiltchikow's cavalry, some 22,000 men.

In the evening after the battle the centre of gravity of the French army had been transferred from the Reims to the Soissons road, and there could now no longer be any idea of anticipating Blücher at Laon. He must be followed directly and his rearguard defeated if, as Napoleon assumed, he was in full retreat on Avesnes. The idea of Woronzow being merely a rearguard which could be easily brushed aside was soon found to be false, and Napoleon had to call up practically everything he had on the Reims road, except the Polish lancers at Festieux, and Marmont and Arrighi at Berry-au-Bac. He actually engaged a number very little more than equal to Woronzow's, but he still had a reserve of about 8000 men in the divisions of Christiani and Poret de Morvan.[7] He had 102 guns against 96.

The strength of the Russian position consisted in the fact that it was approached in front by a narrow neck which could be effectively swept by artillery fire, whilst the flanks rested on steep slopes, in the case of the left an almost precipitous slope. The one objection on this side was that the slope was so steep as to leave a considerable amount of ground "dead" to artillery fire from above. On the right the slopes were less steep, but still, by the route taken by Nansouty, very difficult for cavalry. There was a gentler slope up the end of the spur, but it would have entailed a considerable circuit, and that in a direction where the allies had some cavalry on the watch.

We have already shown how Ney erred in throwing in his infantry on the flank without waiting for orders, and, still worse, without artillery at first. The consequence of his not waiting for the frontal attack to develop was that Boyer de Rebeval's division, instead of being used for the frontal attack as intended, had to be sent round to the flank to save Ney from utter disaster. The "evènement" at Craonne is highly characteristic of Napoleon. He

---

7. These were quite large divisions of 3300 and 4800 respectively for this campaign. Pierre Boyer's single brigade division was less than 1900 strong; Meunier's less than 1000, Curial's just over 1000.

launches against the enemy's centre, already exhausted by five or six hours' fighting, a storm of grape and canister from 88 guns, followed immediately by a charge of the Guard infantry and cavalry. But the Russian troops rarely gave way to panic, and the retreat was carried out in good order.

Blücher's plan for a turning movement was good in conception but badly executed. His order, fetching Winzingerode back six miles late at night before starting him on his march, to Festieux, was almost as much to blame for the failure in execution as Winzingerode's slowness next day. What Blücher should apparently have done was to send Winzingerode's cavalry direct across the Lette by Cerny and Chamomile, and to send back orders to the rest of the cavalry detailed to pass at Chevregny and join Winzingerode's rear at Chamomile by Trucy, Grandelain, and Colligis. That would have left the crossing clear for Kleist when he followed.

Even then, it is by no means certain that the movement would have had all the effect that Blücher hoped. The Emperor would have been able to oppose to it the troops of Marmont, Arrighi, and Bordessoulle, brought up from Berry-au-Bac, besides the divisions of Christiani and Poret de Morvan which he did not actually engage against Woronzow. Still it would probably have brought him to a standstill and he would not have been before Laon on the 9th. That, as we shall see, would perhaps have been fortunate for him. Blücher seems to have made another mistake in leaving Sacken's infantry doing nothing at Froidmont, instead of bringing it up within supporting distance of Woronzow. Had he done so, Craonne might not even have been the hard-won victory for Napoleon that it was. The French at Craonne took not a single gun or other trophy.

In the night of the 7th-8th Bülow was in position at Laon. Yorck had reached Leuilly through Etouvelles; Winzingerode and Kleist were at Festieux; Sacken and Langeron (including the garrison of Soissons) on the march for Laon.

During this night Napoleon, as usual now, allowing the wish to be father to the thought, persuaded himself that the enemy was retreating in utter disorder by Laon, at which place he would have nothing but a rearguard which could be easily ejected and pushed northwards. The Emperor's first orders on the 8th sent a regiment of cavalry to ascertain if Soissons had been evacuated, and if so to recall the old garrison from Compiègne.

The advance on Laon was continued, on Napoleon's side, by Ney's three divisions, preceded as advance guard by Belliard with the cavalry of Colbert, Laferrière, Roussel d'Urbal and Grouvel.[8] This advance was by Chavignon, Urcel and Chivy. Arrighi, Marmont, and Bordessoulle were to move simultaneously by the Reims-Laon road. The rest of the army would stand, for the moment, about L'Ange Gardien ready to march on Laon, Soissons, or Reims, as circumstances might require. At daybreak Soissons was found to be evacuated, though the news only reached Napoleon about 1 p.m.

Belliard, forcing the passage of the Lette at Chavignon, found himself stopped by superior forces before Etouvelles and had to wait in a thick mist for Ney's infantry, which only came up at 2 p.m., and, after having failed to take the place up to 5 p.m., was recalled to Urcel.

Notwithstanding this, the Emperor still averred that there was only a rearguard to deal with at Laon. He decided to attack Etouvelles in the dark hours of the morning of the 9th, and, having taken it, to send Ney and Mortier forward to surprise the supposed rearguard at Laon, on which place Marmont would also march by the Reims road.

For the night of the 8th-9th the main body of the French army stood between L'Ange Gardien and Urcel. Napoleon spent the night at Chavignon with the Old Guard and with Charpentier.[9] Marmont had been slack again, said it was too late to march that evening to Corbény, and put off his march till next morning.

---

8. Commanding in place of Watier in disgrace.
9. Charpentier, a native of Soissons who had spent part of his youth at Laon, had special local knowledge.

CHAPTER 8

Laon and Reims

It was 1 a.m. on the 9th when Ney began his advance on Etouvelles and Chivy. Gourgaud, with two battalions of Old Guard and 300 cavalry, had been sent during the night from Chavignon by Chaillevois and Chailvet to co-operate with Ney's frontal attack by turning the enemy's right. At 1.30 a.m., there being no signs of Gourgaud, Ney started his attack, headed by 400 volunteers of Pierre Boyer's brigade. The Russians at Etouvelles, surprised and turned by the volunteers, surrendered without much fighting, but at Chivy it was different. Gourgaud's turning movement had been retarded by the badness of the road, aggravated by a heavy fall of snow in the night. It was not till 4 a.m. that Ney got possession of Chivy, and Belliard's cavalry was sent forward to try and surprise Laon.

At 5.30 a.m. Gourgaud's cavalry arrived before the suburb of Semilly, to find the enemy fully on his guard. The same state of affairs was found by Belliard's cavalry at Clacy, and at the suburb of Ardon. Everywhere they were met by a violent fire of musketry. Clearly Laon was not to be taken by a rush. Gourgaud's two battalions took post in a little wood between Chivy and Semilly.

At 7 a.m. Mortier began to arrive at Chivy, and relieved Ney, who marched against Semilly, Mortier taking the direction of Ardon. Ney at first succeeded in getting into Semilly, but was soon driven out by a counter-attack. It was not till 11 a.m. that he again got into the suburb, to be driven out once more. At 9 a.m. Poret de Morvan, of Mortier's corps, had stormed Ardon, and was pushing troops against the southern slopes of the hill of Laon, whence, about 11 a.m., they were driven back on to the plain.

We must now return to Blücher. The old man was suffering severely from fever and from incipient ophthalmia, but he had not the slightest idea of making off northwards beyond Laon as Napoleon had believed.

Unlike most of the other allied generals, he was never afraid of Napoleon, and now, in the advantageous position of Laon, with an army two-and-a-half times Napoleon's numbers, he was more than ready to fight.

His army had as its centre Bülow's 17,000 men holding the strong position of the hill of Laon, and the suburbs of Semilly and Ardon.

On the open plain, on the right facing Clacy, was Winzingerode's corps still, after the losses at Craonne, 25,000 strong. On the left, Yorck and Kleist with about 24,000 were about Athies, across the Reims road. Langeron and Sacken with 36,000 were in reserve behind Laon.[1]

Blücher, too ill to sit a horse, posted himself on the southwest corner of the hill whence, when the mist lifted about 11 a.m., he had a magnificent view of the battlefield spread at his feet.

At that hour Poret de Morvan still held Ardon with difficulty. Behind him, about Leuilly, were Christiani's Old Guard division, Roussel d'Urbal's dragoons, and Pac's Polish lancers.

Pierre Boyer was in front of Semilly, with Meunier and Cu-

---

1. See *Supra*, p. 115 for Blücher's numbers on the 4th March. Since then he had lost about 5000 men at Craonne and perhaps another 2000 at Soissons on the 5th, at Heurtebise and Vauclerc on the 6th and on the 8th. He must still have had at least 103,000 men. Of the 48,000 Napoleon had on the 4th, he had lost 1500 at Soissons on the 5th, at least 5500 at Craonne on the 6th and perhaps 500 on the 8th. We have also to deduct 1000 for De France at Reims and the cavalry regiment at Soissons—in all 8500. That leaves him 40,000, of whom about 30,000 were with himself and 10,000 with Marmont. It is difficult to arrive at exact figures, but, looking to the certainly vast disproportion, it is not of vital importance whether Napoleon had with himself 30,000 men, or as Houssaye (195) says, only 27,000.

rial in reserve. Colbert's and Letort's cavalry, and Gourgaud's two battalions watched the woods between Semilly and Chivy, a very insignificant force against Winzingerode's 25,000 men beyond Clacy.

That general had been ordered to make a vigorous attack on the French left, and to send Wassiltchikow by the foot of the hills on his right to turn it by Mons-en-Laonnois. His execution of the order was very feeble; for the cavalry which he sent forward was repulsed, and the infantry division he sent to Clacy appears to have confined itself to helping Bülow once more to drive Ney from Semilly at noon. It was, however, driven back by Curial, though Pierre Boyer again failed in another attack on Semilly.

At the same time, Poret de Morvan was driven from Ardon, but succeeded in getting back there, thanks to a charge by Roussel d'Urbal and Pac on the left flank of the Prussians following him. An attempt to get into communication with Marmont failed. The hour was about 1 p.m. Napoleon had only now come up to Chivy to find he had before him something very much more than the rearguard he had prophesied. Ney and Mortier were only just holding their own. As for Marmont, the strong west wind prevented any sounds of his action reaching the Emperor's ears.

Had Blücher, reinforcing Winzingerode and Bülow with the reserves of Sacken and Langeron, advanced boldly on his right, he would almost certainly have carried away the French left. But he, too, suffered under a delusion, believing Napoleon's attack to be only a feint, and that the main attack was coming by the Reims road. He accordingly moved his reserves leftwards.

As soon as he realized the true state of affairs, Napoleon ordered Charpentier and Friant up to Chivy.

The country in which the Emperor stood was so wooded and marshy that there was little scope for anything but infantry. It was only where Winzingerode stood, north of Clacy, that the terrain was suitable for all arms. Napoleon, deciding to attack the allied right, would presently have available Charpentier and

Friant (about 13,500 infantry), besides 3500 cavalry and 106 guns which were of little value till Clacy was passed. It was 4.30 p.m. when Charpentier was ready. By 6.30 p.m. he had stormed the village from the south and east, but even here it was not possible to bring into action sufficient guns to oppose Winzingerode's powerful artillery.

During Charpentier's attack on Clacy, Ney had failed once more to take Semilly, and Poret de Morvan, mortally wounded himself, was driven from Ardon.

Darkness had fallen before, at 7 p.m., the fighting was over for the night, and the Emperor returned to Chavignon.

Mortier held Semilly with outposts in front from the Ardon Brook to join Pierre Boyer who was in front of Semilly, with Meunier and Curial joining him to Charpentier at Clacy. Charpentier extended towards Laniscourt, along the right bank of the brook which flows at the foot of the hills from Molinchart to Clacy. Detachments of cavalry continued the line beyond Laniscourt. In reserve were Friant's Old Guard and Letort and Colbert at Chivy and Etouvelles. Exelmans and Grouvel returned to Chavignon with Napoleon.

The allies were in close contact all along this line. They had a detachment in Bruyères opposed to French cavalry in Nouvion-le-Vineux.

The results of a desperate day's fighting had been practically nil. Beyond the capture of Etouvelles, Chivy and Clacy, Napoleon had gained nothing. But the battle on the opposite wing was by no means over. Marmont had encountered no real opposition up to Festieux, which he reached at 10 a.m. Here, though the west wind bore to him the sounds of Napoleon's battle, he waited for the mist to clear before resuming his advance half an hour after noon. After some fighting, he had taken Athies with Arrighi's division by 5 p.m. The enemy having retired on Chambry, Marmont bivouacked for the night, and, at 7 p.m., without troubling to assure himself that the arrangements for protection in presence of the enemy were satisfactory, he went off to spend the night at Eppes.

A detachment of 600 infantry and 400 cavalry, under Colonel Fabvier, was sent towards Bruyères to establish communication with the Emperor.

Marmont's front was in contact with the enemy on the line Sauvoir Farm—Athies Mill—Mannoise Farm, but Arrighi's outposts were weak, very tired, and without special instructions. The guns in the park, south of Athies, were still unlimbered, as they had been at the end of the action, and no patrols were sent out to watch the enemy. Bordessoulle's cavalry, also insufficiently protected, kept no watch on the numerous Prussian squadrons north-east of Athies. Everywhere Marmont's troops were off their guard, the men warming themselves by the campfires, for it was freezing and the plain was covered with snow.

Marmont had scarcely reached Eppes at 7.30 p.m., when Arrighi's two brigades were attacked by strong Prussian columns. The surprise was complete. Athies was taken, and the two battalions holding it cut up. Arrighi's whole division was soon in flight, and his guns could not be got away owing to their being unlimbered. Bordessoulle's men were scarcely mounted when the whole mass of Prussian cavalry fell upon them from the Athies-Eppes road.

The French cavalry, completely broken, fled through the defeated infantry of Arrighi. Then the Prussian cavalry got ahead of the 6th corps as it was making for Festieux, cutting off its retreat, killing the artillery and park horses, so that all Marmont's *matériel* was helpless.

Marmont rejoined his troops and did his best to restore order. But nothing could prevent a general rout and flight towards Festieux, under constant fire from the Prussian infantry and artillery, and charges by their cavalry.

The situation was relieved by two incidents: Colonel Fabvier, hearing that Mortier had lost Ardon, and also of the disaster to Marmont, was on his way back to Festieux by Veslud, which he reached about 10 p.m. He vigorously attacked the enemy who had reached the place. At the same time, the Prussian cavalry, trying to head off Marmont at Festieux, found there 100 veterans of the Old Guard, halted for the night on their way to the army. These old soldiers promptly organized a defence of the village with the aid of two of Marmont's guns which had escaped. The Prussians were beaten off, and, thanks to this and to Fabvier's diversion, the Prussian pursuit stopped at Maison Rouge. At Corbény some sort of order was restored, but it was only at Berry-au-Bac that Marmont could commence reorganizing his column, which had lost 3500 men, 45 out of 55 guns, 131 *caissons*, and most of its wheeled transport.

Such was the disastrous "*Hurrah d'Athies*" as the French call this night surprise. Marmont must bear the whole responsibility for the neglect of protective arrangements which left his force in contact with a powerful enemy with outposts which, in addition to being weak, were much too close to the main body which they covered. The marshal had failed to make any provision for a counter-attack in case of being attacked, and he had failed in his duty by seeking comfortable quarters in Eppes before assuring himself that all was well in front.

Yet, for the whole failure on the 9th, a failure which would have resulted in disaster had the allies been commanded by a general of Napoleon's calibre, the blame must rest on the Emperor. His obstinate persistence in his belief that Blücher was retreating northwards, leaving only a rearguard at Laon, led him to make his extremely dangerous advance in two columns, separated by an almost impassable country.

To realize the risk he ran, it is only necessary to think what he would have done himself had he and Blücher changed places. He would probably have realized that the attack on the western wing was the main one. He would have contained Marmont with Yorck and Kleist, and hurled the whole of the remaining 80,000 allies on the 30,000 of the French left. Who can doubt the result?

The fact was that Blücher had a very exaggerated conception of Napoleon's strength, believing him to have 60,000 men.

The blame attachable to Napoleon is not that he deliberately attacked an army of such strength that he could have no reasonable hope of victory, but that he persisted in a false hypothesis, according to which he was only going to have to do with the rear guard of a demoralized and retreating army. We shall see something analogous to this a few days later at Arcis-sur-Aube. The credit for the design of the night attack appears to be due to Yorck, for the excellent execution of it to his troops.

On the morning of the 10th Napoleon, before he knew of Marmont's disaster, had ordered a general attack by both columns, Marmont's and his own. He was by way of still believing in Blüchers retreat on Avesnes. When, at last, he was convinced regarding Marmont's defeat, he shifted his ground, and, maintaining that Blücher must have weakened his right and centre in order to strengthen his left against Marmont, held that, if he himself held firm, he would compel Blücher to abandon Laon, or, at the worst, to give up the pursuit of Marmont.

Curiously enough, this desperate measure did have the effect which the Emperor had no reasonable right to expect.

That it did so was mainly due to the physical breakdown of the Prussian Field-marshal. The old man, racked with fever, and rapidly becoming temporarily blind with ophthalmia, had with difficulty kept himself going at all on the 9th. At midnight he was still able to issue orders, sending Yorck and Kleist after Marmont on Berry-au-Bac, to pass the Aisne there, or, if the bridge there were broken, at Neufchatel higher up, to get into communication with St. Priest towards Reims, and to throw themselves on the right of the French army as it retreated on Fismes.

Sacken was to follow to Corbény, and thence pass the Aisne either at Berry-au-Bac or between it and Vailly. Langeron to go by Bruyères to Heurtebise and the plateau of Craonne, awaiting orders there, but sending his pontoons on to Maizy to prepare a bridge over the Aisne. He would receive orders later, according to circumstances, either to cross at Maizy and move on Braisne, or to march westwards by the plateau on L'Ange Gardien. Bülow and Winzingerode to follow the Emperor.

Had these orders been carried out, Napoleon would have been in an almost desperate situation; but Blücher had reached the end of his tether, and was compelled to delegate his command temporarily to Gneisenau.

If Gneisenau was far superior to Blücher as a strategist, he lacked the strong personality of his chief, which had enabled him, since the union of the armies on the 4th, to keep in check the smouldering animosities and jealousies which existed, not only between Prussians and Russians, but even between the Prussians of Bülow and their fellow-countrymen of Blücher's corps, whom they affected to consider as worn out and useless. Gneisenau's position was one of great responsibility, and, in the event of Blücher's complete disablement for the command, he was liable at any moment to be superseded by the senior corps commander, who happened to be Langeron. Langeron's dread of being called to the responsibilities of chief command is shown by his rather brutal remark as he left Blücher's sick chamber, "In God's name let us carry this corpse with us."

Gneisenau, returning to Blücher's observation post of the previous day, saw that the Emperor was not yet retreating. He dreaded the responsibility of carrying out the bold but undoubtedly correct manoeuvre ordered at midnight. Notwithstanding the remonstrances of the staff, he, about 8 a. m., cancelled those orders. Langeron and Sacken were now to hold fast till the enemy disclosed his intentions. Yorck and Kleist, pursuing Marmont with light cavalry only, were to stop at Corbény. Bülow and Winzingerode were to prepare to meet the general attack which Napoleon seemed to be preparing.

Gneisenau's hesitation and weakness saved Napoleon. The operations of the day may be briefly disposed of Woronzow, advancing with infantry against Clacy, was as much unable to get into it in the face of the French artillery and infantry fire as Charpentier was unable to advance beyond it. The deadlock here continued till 2 p.m., when Gneisenau decided to reinforce Woronzow by troops from Bülow's corps which had hitherto stood idle in Laon. Napoleon, observing these movements, still affected to believe in the enemy's approaching retreat. Charpentier was ordered to break out from Clacy, Ney to attack Semilly once more, and Mortier to storm Ardon. Charpentier was soon stopped by the Russian fire, and Mortier equally failed before Ardon. Ney sent Curial forward against Semilly, which he succeeded in taking, and even pushed up the slopes of the hill of Laon. Thence, however, he was driven back through Semilly by a fearful artillery fire, and by a Prussian counter-attack with the bayonet.

It was 4 p.m. when the reconnaissances of Drouot and Belliard at last convinced Napoleon, against his will, that the offensive was hopeless, and decided him to order the retreat on Soissons.

Meanwhile, on the allies' side, Gneisenau's orders had been received by the corps commanders with dismay. Yorck in particular attributed them to Gneisenau's personal disagreement with him. One after another came envoys from Yorck and Kleist, including Grolmann (Kleist's Chief of staff), imploring permission to advance and cut off Napoleon from Soissons. The only result was that Gneisenau made his orders still harder to bear, by directing Kleist and Yorck to fall back on Athies. Everyone, including Müffling, thought the cancellation of Blücher's orders a fatal mistake; but there was nothing for it but to obey.

Thanks to Gneisenau's hesitation, Napoleon's retreat on Soissons was practically unmolested, and on the nth he was able to take up a position at and north of Soissons with the 24,000 men left him after the loss of some 6000 before Laon on his own wing. Marmont was reduced to little over 6000 men and ten guns. He was at Berry-au-Bac on the 10th, but announced his intention of retreating on Fismes next day. He got there, but was met by an order from Napoleon to return at once to Berry-au-Bac, as he had only light troops facing him.

Napoleon, in taking up an offensive position north of Soissons, hoped to draw the enemy on himself, relieving Marmont, and leaving the way open for the garrisons he had summoned from the fortresses of the Meuse and the Moselle to join that marshal. On the 11th and 12th the Emperor was busy issuing orders for the defence of Soissons, for the march of the north-eastern garrisons, and to Broussier at Strasburg to break out, and, gathering up the garrisons in that neighbourhood, to harass Schwarzenberg's communications. Gneisenau's position, meanwhile, grew more and more difficult.

The jealousies and quarrels, kept in check by Blücher's personality, were now rampant; the troops, very short of food, were marauding in all directions, and had to be widely scattered to subsist. On the evening of the 12th Bülow was beyond La Fère, Langeron at Coucy-le-Chateau, Sacken at Chavignon, Winzingerode at Laon, Kleist at Bouconville, Yorck between Corbény and Berry-au-Bac.

Finally, Yorck, taking umbrage at the supposed personal animosity of Gneisenau against himself, took the extraordinary step of throwing up his command, on the ground of ill-health, and actually starting for Brussels. He was only stopped by a personal appeal from Blücher. On this day (12th) St. Priest, from the direction of Châlons, retook Reims from the garrison of National Guards.

When Napoleon heard of this he saw his way to an easy victory, which might to some extent restore his lost prestige. From all sides bad news was pouring in on him. Macdonald was retreating on Paris; Augereau was falling back in the south; Eugene in Italy was losing ground to Murat; the allies were on the point of breaking up the Congress of Châtillon, and had tightened the bond uniting themselves by the Treaty of Chaumont; Paris was becoming daily more discontented, and everybody, the Regency included, was demanding peace on the allies' terms; the National Guards in Paris had refused to join the army. Something must be done to restore confidence in the Emperor. Soissons was already in a position for defence, thanks to the energy of Gérard, [2] the new commandant.

Before starting, as he now proposed, for the recapture of Reims, Napoleon had to reorganize the shattered remains of his army.

To Sebastiani were given the cavalry divisions of Colbert and

---

2. Not to be confused with the leader of the 2nd corps.

Letort, with which he was to march in the night of the 12th-13th to Braisne. Ney, with the remains of Pierre Boyer's single brigade and two other regiments, [3] was also to start at once, so as to be before Reims early on the 13th. Mortier was left about Soissons with the divisions of Charpentier, Boyer de Rebeval, Curial, Poret de Morvan, Christiani, and Meunier, and the cavalry of Roussel d'Urbal, Pac, and a regiment of miscellaneous squadrons. The Emperor estimated Mortier's strength at 8000 or 9000 infantry and 4000 cavalry. The garrison of Soissons, if Mortier had to leave it, was to be 1500 men, including some 400 or 500 lame men of the Guard.

Friant was to march in the early morning for Reims. Marmont also to march at 6 a.m. with his own command and Defrance, who had escaped from Reims,[4] leaving a rearguard at Berry-au-Bac. He would be the advance guard.

St. Priest, meanwhile, had no suspicion of the storm which was about to burst on him. Even when Bordessoulle and Defrance, followed by Ricard's infantry, drove in his advanced troops, he did not awake to the situation, and took up a bad position west of Reims, with the city and the Vesle behind him. It was 4 p.m. before the Emperor was up in full force. Then St. Priest recognized, from the vigour of the attack led by Marmont, supported by Ney, Friant, and Letort, that he had to deal with Napoleon in person. As he was organizing his retreat, he was mortally wounded by a round shot. [5] Nothing could resist the French attack, and, though Marmont was delayed in taking the Soissons gate of the city, the remains of St. Priest's corps was driven to Berry-au-Bac which it reached in the morning of the 14th. It had suffered a loss of 3000 men and twenty-three guns. A few considerations of time and space will serve to show that this operation against Reims was carried out with all the energy of Napoleon's best days. From Soissons to Reims by Fismes is

---

3. The 122nd just arrived from Paris and the Regiment of the Vistula, the former garrison of Soissons.
4. *Corr.* 21,475.
5. Napoleon says the gunner who fired the shot was the same as he who had killed Moreau at Dresden, which may or may not be true. *Corr.* 21,478.

about forty-three miles. Napoleon's orders to Berthier are dated 6 p.m. on the 12th. Allowing for issue of separate orders, etc., it is hardly possible that Ney's infantry could have started before 8 p.m. Within twenty hours they were ready for battle at a distance which may be taken as about equal to that from Paddington to Pangbourne. Still more remarkable was Friant's feat; for he was to start only at 2 a.m. on the 13th, and in fourteen hours he had covered forty miles.

The attack on St. Priest was a surprise, and, though Napoleon had between 20,000 and 25,000 men coming up, he appears only to have had to engage 8000 or 10,000 against St. Priest's 14,500. It was the assembly with such rapidity of Napoleon's troops that was the triumph. Gneisenau had just declared such a move to be beyond the capabilities of the French.

In addition to the political effects in Paris of this victory, it had placed Napoleon across the communications between the two allied armies.

Having arrived at the conclusion of a distinct manoeuvre, the second since Brienne against Blücher, it will be convenient to take the opportunity to make some remarks on it. The first thing to be noticed is Napoleon's reluctance, in the end of February, to believe that Blücher could be moving on Paris. Perhaps the greatest mistake he made in this campaign was in underestimating the determination and the energy of the Prussian Field-marshal, and the capacity of his staff. Napoleon was never very far wrong in his estimate of Schwarzenberg, but he seems to have failed to recognize fully how very different an opponent Blücher was. If the latter was always ready to obey orders loyally when they reached him, he rejoiced when he found himself so far separated from headquarters that he could not be harassed with them.

In such circumstances, he could give rein to his own energetic ideas. He had gained a great start before Napoleon began his movement. He had lost much of it when the Emperor reached Château-Thierry, but he once more regained some of it when Napoleon was hung up on the left bank of the Marne from want of the means of passage. Napoleon, at this period, was constantly complaining of the want of a pontoon train. It certainly deprived him of many chances.

Marmont and Mortier had done extremely well with their small force on the Ourcq, but nevertheless, by the evening of the 3rd March Napoleon had no longer any chance of preventing Blücher from crossing the Aisne, or of cutting him off, as he had hoped to do when he was close on his heels at Château-Thierry.

He knew that Blücher had been joined by Winzingerode and must exceed himself in numerical strength by at least 50 *per cent*. He did not know that Bülow also was in touch, and that Blücher had now more than double his strength.

Henceforward Napoleon allowed imagination to master facts. He kept persuading himself, without any sufficient grounds, that Blücher was in full flight northwards, that he would be able to drive the army of Silesia beyond Laon, and, by re-arming that place and Soissons, to prevent its approaching Paris, whilst he went off to pick up his garrisons, and to attack Schwarzenberg in conjunction with Macdonald. Again he misjudged both the resources and the energy of Blücher. He had to abandon his advance by the Reims road in order to fight the battle of Craonne against Woronzow, who might be the rearguard in Blücher's retreat on Laon, or, on the other hand, might be the advanced guard of an eastward march.

When, next day, he found Blücher retreating on Laon, he once more deluded himself with the idea that he would find nothing but a rearguard at Laon. The resistance incurred by Ney at Etouvelles might have given him pause, but again on the 9th we find him keeping back his main body at Chavignon, whilst Ney and Mortier on the one side, Marmont on the other, advanced concentrically, hopelessly separated from one another, to sweep away the supposed rearguard and surprise Laon. The surprise was all the other way, for the Emperor found he was opposed, not to a rearguard, but to the whole of Blücher's army.

Even on the 10th he at first seems to have thought he could

compel Blücher to leave Laon, and it was only later in the day that he continued the action merely with the object of showing a bold front and preventing the general advance which must have ruined him. His resolution is admirable, and it had the effect of imposing on the allies as he hoped.

Still, that he was able to hold on at Soissons till he marched thence on Reims was largely due to Blücher's illness, and Gneisenau's inaction consequent thereon. Had Yorck and Kleist been allowed to follow up Marmont, and to gather in St. Priest when they had crossed the Aisne at Berry-au-Bac, the movement on Reims would have been impossible, and Napoleon must have been forced to retreat, either on Paris, or towards Macdonald at Provins.

Blücher's conduct of the campaign is highly commended by Clausewitz and Müffling. If he made a serious mistake, it was in waiting too long at Château-Thierry, and in trying to deal a blow at Marmont and Mortier on the Ourcq with Kleist's insufficient force. He would perhaps have been wiser, once he found Napoleon was on his heels, to concentrate his energies on joining Winzingerode and Bülow, with whose strength added to his own he would have been in a position to advance without fear, and at the moment that suited him best, against Napoleon's greatly inferior army.

His separation from Schwarzenberg in the beginning of February has been severely criticized by Clausewitz. At that time, Blücher, with a little over 50,000 men, including all the reinforcements he was likely to receive for the present, was going off alone with the possibility of being followed by Napoleon with forces not much inferior. In the end of February it was quite different; for he would be able to join reinforcements bringing him up to over 100,000 men, a force greater than Napoleon could oppose to him and to Schwarzenberg.

CHAPTER 9

Arcis-Sur-Aube

Napoleon, having retaken Reims on the 13th March, spent the three following days there in organizing his next movement. Gneisenau was still playing a role of complete inactivity at Laon, and thereby affording the Emperor the breathing space he badly required.

We know that the Emperor's design now was to gather up his eastern and north-eastern garrisons, and with them to return upon Schwarzenberg. Of these, Janssens, with 3000 men from the Ardennes garrisons, was able to join Ney as that marshal marched from Reims to Châlons, which latter fell into his hands without resistance.

On the other side, Colbert drove Tettenborn from Epernay, whence he had recently been operating by raids on Napoleon's rear.

The Emperor would fain have gone off at once to meet the garrisons in Lorraine, but, unfortunately for him, Schwarzenberg had, during the manoeuvre against Blücher, pushed Macdonald so far on the road to Paris that, if Napoleon went eastwards, the allies might be in Paris before he could return. He saw that Schwarzenberg must first be brought back eastwards, and he was in some doubt as to how to do it best.

The plan he eventually decided on was to leave Marmont and Mortier with about 21,000 men to contain Blücher, whilst he himself moved against Schwarzenberg. For this purpose he would have some 24,000, including 4500 reinforcements about

125

to reach him from Paris under Lefebvre-Desnoettes.[1] He had three possible directions in which to march:

(1) On Arcis-sur-Aube, so as to reach Troyes in Schwarzenberg's rear on the 20th;

(2) on Provins, to join Macdonald in front of Schwarzenberg;

(3) direct on Meaux. He decided on the first, rejecting the second summarily on account of its bad crossroads, and the third because he held it to have no advantage beyond bringing him close to Paris. The first he chose because "it is the boldest, and its results are incalculable."

Before following his movement, we must recount briefly what had happened to Macdonald and his lieutenant, Oudinot, since we left them on the 26th February. Oudinot, on the 26th February, had not acted with much intelligence. His orders were to "move on Bar-sur-Aube." They reached him at Vendœuvre, and it is by no means clear why he should have gone round by Dolancourt instead of direct. He was pursuing a very superior enemy, and it was certainly not his duty to contemplate a pitched battle. The enemy might turn back against him at any moment, in which case his duty would be to delay a fresh advance by retiring fighting.

There was nothing in his orders to require him to carry the greater part of his army across the Aube, and he was certainly bound to take a position for the night which would not be open to surprise. He would have done well to remain behind the Aube, with a strong rearguard in Bar-sur-Aube,[2] employing Kellermann's cavalry to obtain "*beaucoup de nouvelles*," as the Emperor's orders required. Instead of that, he kept half his cavalry at Spoy for facilities of forage; he had four divisions of infantry in the valley on the right bank, with the Aube close behind them,

---

1. Napoleon expected 11,000, but 3000 infantry and 1500, cavalry were all that reached him.

2. The Emperor's orders of next morning show that this is what Oudinot was meant to do.

whilst Pacthod was at Dolancourt and Duhesme at Bar.

There was little to watch the hills above the valley, nothing to watch the forest of Sevigny, by which his left might be turned, and he had most of his artillery behind the river. He had full warning of the probability of an offensive return in an attack by the Bavarians on Bar in the evening, and in information brought in by the inhabitants.

Despite all Napoleon's precautions, Schwarzenberg seems to have realized that the Emperor was leaving his front. Blücher had written to the King of Prussia, on the 25th, that Napoleon was about to move against himself, leaving only two corps in front of Schwarzenberg. The letter seems to have been written in the hope of stopping the retreat of the army of Bohemia; for Blücher could not know what Napoleon had not really yet decided. The letter had its effect; for Schwarzenberg decided to attack Oudinot on the 27th, holding him in front with Wrede towards Bar, whilst Wittgenstein turned his left.

Into the details of the battle we need not enter. The end of it was that Oudinot was badly beaten, with a loss of 3500 men. He had 27,500 men available against 26,000 allies, but, owing to his faulty position, he could only bring 18,000 into action. The only marvel was that he escaped so lightly, and was able to fall back towards Troyes, a movement which, of course, entailed a retreat of Macdonald on the same place. By the night of the 4th March Schwarzenberg had again occupied Troyes. Macdonald was suffering severely from the gradual dissolution of his army by sickness, desertion, and straggling.

By the 17th March the 42,000 men left by Napoleon (including Oudinot's command) had dwindled to 30,000. At Troyes Schwarzenberg again stopped till the 12th March. On the 10th the Tsar, resenting Schwarzenberg's inaction, had sent for him to Chaumont. Schwarzenberg, who knew nothing of what had happened in Blücher's direction, submitted a long memorandum, setting forth three hypotheses:

(1) That part of Napoleon's army had been beaten by Blücher, and the Emperor was voluntarily falling back on

Paris;

(2) Napoleon, having beaten Blücher, was marching against the right of the Bohemian army by Châlons;

(3) Napoleon, having fought no great battle, was marching as above. It was only on the 11th, just as Schwarzenberg left Chaumont, that news of the battle of Craonne arrived from St. Priest.

Schwarzenberg was in a pitiful state of hesitation.

"I have no news," he wrote on the 12th March, "and I avow that I tremble. If Blücher suffers a defeat, how can I give battle myself; for, if I am beaten, what a triumph for Napoleon, and what a humiliation for the Sovereigns to have to repass the Rhine at the head of a beaten army!"[3]

So long as he was ignorant of what had happened to Blücher, he dared not advance on Paris, exposing his right and his long line of communications to a return of a possibly victorious Napoleon.

It was only on the 14th that a serious attempt was made to drive Macdonald from behind the Seine, when Wrede bombarded Bray and Rajewski,[4] crossing at Pont-sur-Seine, marched on Villenauxe.

That night came news of the battle of Laon, and for the next day or two Schwarzenberg acted with somewhat more energy, so that on the evening of the 16th Macdonald stood with the main body of his army behind Provins, with Pacthod at Montereau, and Allix and Souham[5] on the Loing.

Here Schwarzenberg's advance stopped, in consequence of news just received of St. Priest's defeat at Reims, and the reoccupation of Châlons by Napoleon's troops.

Allied headquarters at this time were anything but a happy family. The freedom with which Schwarzenberg was criticized, by the Russians especially, is shown by a letter to Toll from an

---

3. *Janson*, 2., 220.
4. Commanding the 6th corps *vice* Wittgenstein retired.
5. Souham commanded a weak force of newly formed troops.

*aide-de-cam*p of the Tsar in which he speaks of the commander-in-chief as, "*cette malheureuse verdure, ou plutôt ordure viennoise.*" [6]

Yet the Tsar himself was in such a disturbed and uncertain state of mind as to lead Wolkonski to write confidentially to Toll: "In a word, we do not know what we want. For the love of God calm us, reassure us. I am wasting all my time in writing in every direction." [7] On the 16th Schwarzenberg had issued no less than three different sets of general orders. Yet he had not lost his head as much as some others. He did not believe, with Radetzky, that Napoleon had been decisively defeated at Laon, and that it was only necessary to advance on Reims in order to crush him between the two armies. He equally did not believe Napoleon was retreating on Paris. In his uncertainty he came to a wise decision, to concentrate at Arcis-sur-Aube and Troyes, a central position whence he could move in any direction when the situation was clearer.

On the 17th Schwarzenberg began to draw his troops together towards Troyes and Arcis. On the 18th he undid this and ordered his army thus:

5th corps on the right bank of the Aube beyond Arcis, occupying Fère Champenoise, and sending advanced guards to Sommesous and Mailly. The Guards and Reserves to descend the right bank towards Dommartin and Donnement.

6th corps to concentrate on the left bank of the Aube, a march which it was not likely to be able to complete in the day.

3rd and 4th corps, Seslawin, and M. Lichtenstein to return to the Seine and Yonne.

The fact appears to be that certain reports, from Tettenborn and from the commandant of Vitry, induced Schwarzenberg to believe that Napoleon was about to move again against Blücher. That such was his belief is stated by Lord Burghersh [8] and Toll. [9] He, therefore, contemplated containing Macdonald with the 3rd

6. Bernhardi, *Toll*. 5. 422
7. *Ibid.*
8. *Memoir of Operations*, etc., p. 206.
9. *Weil*, 3. 389.

and 4th corps, Seslawin, and M. Lichtenstein, whilst, with the rest of the army, he marched from the Aube against the Emperor's rear as he moved on Laon.

When Schwarzenberg was developing this plan, Napoleon was already well on his way southwards in two columns. [10] He had reached Epernay the night before with the right, and now marched by Vertus on Fère Champenoise, whilst Ney with the left moved by Vatry on Sommesous. During the 18th Schwarzenberg's advanced cavalry was met by both columns and driven back. The commander-in-chief had already issued orders for the 19th for a concentration of the 5th and 6th Corps, and the Guards and Reserves north of Arcis, when Kaissarow reported the repulse of his cavalry, and that Napoleon himself was moving south.

The news created consternation at allied headquarters. Schwarzenberg being in bed with gout, the Tsar came over to see him at Arcis. After a somewhat heated interview, orders were issued for Wrede to recross at once to the left bank of the Aube, to defend the passage on the 19th, and to echelon his troops from Arcis to Pougy. The 3rd, 4th and 6th Corps were to fall back on Troyes, leaving

Seslawin to guard the passages at Nogent and Bray as far as possible against Macdonald who had begun to advance again when he felt the relaxation of pressure.

The Guards and Reserves were to fall back on the right bank of the Aube to behind the Voire, remaining thereon the 19th, whilst Wrede, defended the Aube from Arcis to Lesmont. On the 20th, when Wrede got to Lesmont, they would fall back on Trannes and Maisons. Wrede, still leaving parties to watch the enemy on the Aube, would retire by Dienville. Headquarters would be at Pougy on the 19th, and Bar-sur-Aube on the 20th.

On the evening of the 18th the 6th Corps had reached Méry, but still had Eugen of Würtemberg's division at Pont-sur-Seine, and Pahlen near Provins. Wrede was just passing to the left bank

10. Positions evening of 17th.

of the Aube at Arcis. The 4th Corps was also at Méry, with rear-guard at Nogent; where was the 3rd Corps. Seslawin was about Sens and Pont-sur-Yonne. M. Lichtenstein at Tonnerre. Guards and Reserves behind the Voire with light cavalry in front of it. Napoleon's idea on the evening of the 17th seems to have been to march on Arcis, sending Macdonald back to join Marmont and Mortier against Blücher.[11] On the 18th, when he found Wrede in front of him towards Arcis, he decided to cross the Aube at Plancy, and try to catch between two fires the troops facing Macdonald, who was to join himself. After that, he could resume operations against Schwarzenberg's right. He now, at last, had a bridge train, and he hoped to cross the Aube at Plancy at 11 a.m. on the 19th, the Seine at Méry later in the day.

Schwarzenberg was intent on retreating on Bar-sur-Aube, but, as the 3rd, 4th and 6th Corps were still far from Wrede and the Guards and Reserves, it was necessary for Wrede to hold fast on the Aube during the 19th, thus covering the retreat of the left wing on Troyes.

Wrede, watching the Aube from Arcis to Lesmont, below which place all bridges had been broken, had fortified Arcis. Connecting him with the 6th corps at Méry was Kaissarow's cavalry.

Everything being quiet on the Aube in the morning of the 19th, Schwarzenberg believed that Napoleon was making for Brienne and the communications of the army of Bohemia, and that this movement would be accompanied by an advance of Macdonald direct on Troyes. But presently his views were changed when, about 2 p.m., Sebastiani, forcing the passage of the Aube at Plancy, began to prepare bridges for infantry and artillery. Kaissarow was forced back on Pouan, where he was faced by Colbert and Exelmans who, however, made no serious attempt to cross the Barbuisse Brook.[12] Meanwhile, the Emperor himself went with two divisions of cavalry towards Méry, where Letort forded the Seine and captured a fine bridge train

---

11. *Weil*, 3. 403.
12. Positions evening of 19th.

beyond it.

In consequence of Sebastiani's movement, Wrede moved his infantry somewhat forward, so that it held the left bank of the Aube from Pougy to Pouan.

Schwarzenberg was led by these movements to believe that Napoleon had sent Sebastiani to cover the real main movement by Méry on Troyes. The conclusion was wrong, but it led him to a change of plan which was destined to have momentous results, disastrous results for Napoleon. Schwarzenberg, convinced that his right and rear were no longer threatened, now decided to reverse his movement of retreat, to concentrate his army between Troyes and Arcis, and to undertake the offensive against Napoleon in the angle of the Seine and Aube.

Orders issued, at 9 p.m., for the Crown Prince of Würtemberg to take command of the 3rd, 4th and 6th Corps, to leave some troops to watch the Seine about Troyes, and to reach Charmont at 9 a.m. on the 20th, where he would await orders. Wrede was to move towards Plancy, linked to Würtemberg on his left by cavalry. Barclay with the Guards and Reserves was to come over to the left bank at Lesmont, into the country behind Mesnil Lettré.

That night (19th) Napoleon was at Plancy. He had Sebastiani facing Pouan, Letort's and Berckheim's cavalry beyond the Seine, the Guard infantry on both banks of the Aube at Plancy. Ney was on the north bank, with Defrance watching Arcis. Macdonald was still on the right bank of the Seine, from Bray to Pont-sur-Seine, Pacthod at Montereau, Souham and Allix on the Loing. Macdonald's cavalry was forward in the bend of the Seine.

Of the allied army, the 4th and 6th Corps were on the right bank of the Seine opposite Troyes, the 3rd on the left bank. Seslawin was some way behind, and only reached Troyes in the afternoon of the 20th.

It has been assumed that Napoleon deliberately sought the battle of Arcis, a battle in which he was to find the small force he had brought from Reims pitted against the greater part of the army of Bohemia. Even when Macdonald was able to join him he would be greatly inferior in numbers. That was not his intention at all, as is clearly shown by his correspondence.

So far, the enemy had retreated more rapidly than he expected, and, as seemed to be shown by the feeble resistance he encountered on the 19th at Plancy and Méry, Schwarzenberg appeared to be retreating rapidly on Brienne and Bar-sur-Aube. This disappointed the Emperor's hopes of falling on the centre of Schwarzenberg's scattered line of retreat, as he had fallen on Blücher's advance at Champaubert. The enemy's concentration seemed to be completed, and it would have been madness to march against their vast superiority of numbers if they were holding there, which seemed very improbable.

The results of the Emperor's movement by Plancy on the 19th appeared to be:

(1) It had hurried Schwarzenberg's retreat towards Langres.

(2) It had thus disengaged Macdonald and saved Paris.

(3) It had opened the way for Macdonald to join Napoleon.

The Emperor was still intent on gathering up the garrisons, an operation for which he would require at least a week, during which he could meet them by Vitry. During that week he must feel safe against a fresh advance of Schwarzenberg on Paris, which would be completely unguarded on this side. With that time at his disposal, he could call up Marmont and Mortier (20,000), Macdonald (30,000), his own 24,000, forces which, added to the garrisons, would give him quite 90,000 men, a force with which he might well hope to send Schwarzenberg back across the Rhine and then return against Blücher. From his positions of the evening of the 19th, he might march at once for Vitry; but that would have the unfortunate effect of encouraging Schwarzenberg to believe the Emperor was retreating, and inducing him to advance again on Paris.

What Napoleon wanted to do was to first give a further impulse to Schwarzenberg's retreat, which he believed to be in full swing. He could hope to do this by moving up both banks of the Aube to Arcis, where, by the double advance, he would secure the passage, bring back what he had on the left bank to the right, and be able to march on Vitry, followed by Macdonald, with the full assurance that Schwarzenberg was off to Langres. His belief as to Schwarzenberg's intentions was right up to the evening of the 19th, when the Austrian suddenly made up his mind to resume the offensive.[13]

What Napoleon's intentions were is shown by his letter to Clarke of the 20th.[14] "I am going to march on Brienne. I shall neglect Troyes, and shall betake myself in all haste to my fortresses. The line of the army (line of operations) should, it seems to me, be by Sézanne." Later, he says he is starting for Vitry,[15] appearing to abandon the idea of giving a final push to Schwarzenberg by Brienne.

None of his early orders of the 20th indicate any idea of a battle at Arcis. He neither expected nor desired it, and he only moved Ney and the cavalry by the left bank;

(1) in order to facilitate the movement, and;

(2) in order to drive Wrede's rearguard from Arcis, thereby giving fresh impulse to the retreat, and securing the Arcis bridge in co-operation with Defrance and Friant on the north bank, and without the difficulty and delay which must occur in an attack from the north only.

There can be little doubt that Schwarzenberg's sudden change to the offensive must have taken the Emperor quite by surprise. Hitherto, once the army of Bohemia started retreating before Napoleon, it had only stopped when he was no longer in front of it in person. The actual course of events shows how danger-ous it is to rely on the presumed conduct even of an enemy who

---

13. There seems to be no doubt that Schwarzenberg alone was responsible for this change. It was the best thing he did in the campaign. Looking to his previous hesita-tions, it was perhaps the last thing to be expected of him.

14. *Corr.* 21,526.

15. *Corr.* 21,528

has hitherto displayed constant timidity and irresolution.

The French advance by the left bank of the Aube on the morning of the 20th progressed at first without serious difficulty. Before 11 a.m. Sebastiani was in Arcis, from which Wrede's advanced troops had fallen back, and had begun repairing the bridge, which was only slightly damaged. Ney followed him, and his orders to his troops, " to pass to the right bank of the Aube as soon as the bridge is restored," [16] show that a battle on the left bank was not contemplated. His cavalry was to reconnoitre towards L'Huitre and Ramerupt on the right bank.

Meanwhile, Schwarzenberg had issued orders aiming at setting up a line with Wrede on the right about St. Nabord, and the three corps of the left wing extending to Voué, with cavalry protecting their left. The advance would be ordered, about 11 a.m., to proceed due west across the Barbuisse Brook, in the expectation of catching Napoleon in the midst of a flank march on Méry, and cutting him from his bridge at Plancy.

But the Crown Prince, reaching the level of Charmont about 11 a.m. with his three corps, which were much fatigued with recent long marches, understood that the general objective was Plancy. To save having to cross the marshy Barbuisse, he bore leftwards on Premierfait, thus separating himself completely from the right of the army of Bohemia, which was deprived for the whole day of his help. This, and the fact that the French had advanced along the Aube on Arcis, instead of crossing the angle of the Aube and Seine from Plancy to Méry, completely upset Schwarzenberg's scheme.

About midday, Wrede stood with his right thrown forward towards St. Nabord and Torcy-le-Petit, and his left extending towards Voué, whilst Würtemberg was marching away towards Premierfait. Wrede's left was covered by cavalry. The Tsar and the King of Prussia had now joined Schwarzenberg at Mesnil Lettré. The former had been surprised by Schwarzenberg's change to the offensive, and, somewhat inconsistently with his former views, did not approve it. He now believed that Napo-

16. *Weil*, 3. 429.

leon was only amusing the allies on the south bank of the Aube, whilst he marched by the north bank, by Brienne, against their communications towards Bar-sur-Aube. Alexander was very short, almost discourteous, in his treatment of the unfortunate commander-in-chief.

It was 1 p.m. when Napoleon reached Arcis. The rolling downs which surround Arcis on the left bank prevented his seeing anything of the great army which was in the folds behind them, and he obstinately refused credence to the stories of Ney, Sebastiani, and the country folk of an advance of important forces, where he believed there was only a rearguard. He preferred to accept the report of an officer whom he sent out, and who returned, without having gone far enough to see, saying he had only seen 1000 Cossacks. Confirmed by this in his preconceived notions, the Emperor rode to Torcy-le-Grand where Ney was.

At 2 p.m. Schwarzenberg, though he knew his left wing was out of reach towards Premierfait, gave the signal for the general attack which was to have been given at 11 a.m. Wrede's right (Volkmann) advanced against Torcy-le-Grand, whilst the powerful cavalry on his left went forward against the west side of Arcis.

This mass of cavalry was met by Sebastiani with Colbert in first line. Colbert was driven back on Exelmans whose men broke, and the whole of Sebastiani's panic-stricken cavalry fled with the cry of "*sauve qui peut*" towards the bridge at Arcis. There they met, and nearly rode over, the Emperor who, with a few infantry, stood at the approach to the bridge. It was only by immense personal exertion and appeals that he at last succeeded in restoring some order, and again sending forward the terrified cavalry.

Napoleon's position was most critical. He could only just hold on at Arcis with the few infantry he had, and it was only the arrival at the double over the bridge of Friant's leading troops, from the right bank, that saved him.

Ney, meanwhile, was fighting a desperate battle at Torcy-le-Grand. The village was taken and retaken time after time; Ney was actually falling back on Arcis when a reinforcement of three Guard battalions restored the fight. Wrede, too, had reinforced Volkmann, and the struggle continued with the utmost fury. When Miloradowitch came up with 1700 of the Russian Guard, night had fallen, and Ney succeeded in holding the village, where he was heavily bombarded by the Russian guns.

Whilst all this was occurring on the allied right, Würtemberg had met Letort's cavalry, trying to get back from Méry to Arcis, and driven it back into Méry and across the Seine in disorder. The Crown Prince stopped for the night beyond the Barbuisse about Premierfait. The fight on Wrede's front also died gradually away.

But there was still another fight. Napoleon had been joined on his right by 2000 cavalry of Lefebvre-Desnoettes, who had had to leave Hanrion with his worn-out infantry at Plancy. The Emperor now added this cavalry to Sebastiani's, which had been all day engaged with Kaissarow's, and sent the whole forward against the enemy's cavalry between the Barbuisse and the road to Troyes. Sebastiani's charge in the dark was magnificent. Kaissarow went down before him, involving some Bavarian cavalry in his flight. Then, turning to his left, Sebastiani bore down Frimont's cavalry, and was on the point of falling on the left of Wrede's infantry when he was at last stopped by the fire of artillery, and of a Russian grenadier regiment. Then, charged by fresh Russian and Prussian cavalry supported by Frimont's rallied horsemen, he was forced back, though by no means in disorder, to behind Nozay where he spent the night. His men had nobly redeemed their panic of the morning.

That night the allied army occupied a great semicircle in front of Arcis, from Premierfait, through Voué and Mesnil la Comtesse, to Chaudrey.

Napoleon's small force stood on the line Villette-Arcis-Torcy-le-Grand, waiting for Macdonald who had Oudinot between Boulages and Anglure, with cavalry at Plancy; Gérard and Molitor [17] about the mouth of the Aube. Pacthod was still at

---

17. 11th Corps, less Amey's division left at Bray.

Montereau; Souham at Pont-sur-Yonne; Allix at Sens.

The day's fighting had cost the allies over 2000 men against a French loss of probably rather less. They had gained no ground, and had failed to destroy the small force which Napoleon had available.

In order to understand Napoleon's conduct in the ensuing night and on the following morning, it is necessary to realize that he was suffering again, as he had before Laon, from the fatal delusion that the enemy was in full retreat. He still believed that he had only been fighting Wrede, who was covering the retreat of the rest of the army. When, in the evening, he heard of the presence of the enemy towards Premierfait, it seems probable that he took this for the tail end of the army in retreat, and believed that Wrede had fought so strenuously to cover its march towards Bar-sur-Aube.

Had Napoleon not obstinately refused to listen to every report which depicted him as opposed to an immense force, it can hardly be doubted that he would have, in the night, placed himself in safety behind the Aube. Thence he might have operated with his own force up the right bank towards Lesmont and Brienne, leaving Macdonald, as he arrived, to take over the defence of the lower Aube. We know that the Tsar feared such a movement, and, under these circumstances, Schwarzenberg would probably have been compelled to retreat in all haste on Bar. The Tsar knew that there was nothing on the right bank to oppose the Emperor, except Osarowski's light cavalry of the Russian Guard, and Napoleon might well succeed in destroying the Lesmont bridge before the Guard infantry, which was the nearest to it, could get back there.

As it was, the allies, as well as Napoleon, seem to have misunderstood the position, and to have believed that he sought a decisive battle on the left bank.

During the night, Napoleon sent urgent orders to Macdonald to hurry up on Arcis with all his forces.

Schwarzenberg issued orders for the next day at 11 p.m., but somehow it happened that those for the left wing only reached the Crown Prince at 5 a.m., the hour when it was intended that he should be in line on Wrede's left, the whole filling the space from the Aube near Vaupoisson on the right through Mesnil la Comtesse to Voué on the Barbuisse, with cavalry covering its left beyond the brook. As it was, the position was not reached till 10 a.m. There had been delay in the Crown Prince's march; for the French cavalry had attacked Pahlen near Nozay, and had compelled the Prince to protect the flank march of the 3rd, and 4th Corps with the 6th, and to place that corps on his left, instead of on his right as had been ordered, and would naturally have been done. The 3rd became his right, and, as it was weak, owing to part being left at Troyes and on the Seine, cavalry had to be used to fill the space between its right and Wrede's left.

Schwarzenberg's position was very difficult, since the Tsar had plainly shown his disapproval of the offensive movement, and the commander-in-chief himself was now afraid Napoleon might recross the Aube at Arcis and operate up the right bank.

The Emperor had now been joined by the depots of the Guard, by the 2nd and 5th Cavalry Corps, and by Leval's division of the 7th corps. He stood with his right at Pouan, centre at Arcis and left in Torcy.

Schwarzenberg, with his line in place by 10 a.m., hesitated to attack till he saw the position more clearly. Napoleon also did not want to move early, so as to give Macdonald time to arrive. He went to Torcy, but saw nothing but a few *vedettes*, the great line of 74,000 men being hidden from him by the intervening heights. Therefore, he still maintained that the action of the previous day had been nothing but an unusually vigorous rearguard affair. Soon after 10 a. m. he sent Sebastiani forward, followed by Ney's infantry, thus leaving Torcy unguarded.

The sight which met Sebastiani's eyes, as he mounted the plateau at the head of his cavalry, was an alarming one; for now he saw that what the Emperor believed to be a mere rearguard was in reality a great army. Ney, appreciating the position, kept his infantry in column ready to retreat. Pending orders, he and Sebastiani must do what they could, without committing themselves.

The French position was as desperate as could well be conceived. Torcy, the support of their left wing, was abandoned, there were hardly any troops in Arcis, the whole of the little force was being pushed forward against an enemy many times its strength. Had Schwarzenberg pushed boldly on, he must have swept the French bodily into the river and repeated on a small scale the scenes of Leipzig. But it was only at noon, after a council of war, that he made up his mind to issue detailed orders for attack. He still reserved to himself the order for firing the three signal guns announcing that the hour for attack had arrived.

Napoleon, however, was not to be dealt with in this slow methodical manner. As he said before Jena, "At last the veil is torn asunder"; but this time the veil was that created by his own persistent illusions, by his refusal to believe in anything but Schwarzenberg's hurried retreat before the terror of his name.

Once he had seen the falsity of his assumptions, he acted with the decision and promptitude of his best days. He saw that he could not hope to hold out till nightfall against such odds. To retreat through Arcis over a single bridge was a fairly desperate business, but it was the only chance of safety, and orders for it issued at once. Having got his army back to the right bank, the Emperor would carry out his long-decided march by Vitry on St Dizier, rallying his garrisons, raising the country, and transferring the theatre of operations from the plains of Champagne to the mountains of the Vosges and Jura in rear of the allies. This he anticipated would draw them after himself and away from Paris.

The action was to be broken off at once and another bridge of boats thrown at Villette. It was ready by 1.30 p.m. A quarter of an hour later Drouot, with the whole of the Old Guard, was ordered to pass by it and march on Sompuis on the Vitry road. Lefol,[18] followed by the reserve artillery, was already crossing the wooden bridge of Arcis. This column, as well as Milhaud and St. Germain, was to follow Drouot. Letort, from Méry, was

18. In place of Jaussens wounded on the previous day.

to go direct to Sompuis. Macdonald to take position on the right bank, guarding the fords at Boulages and Plancy; he would receive further orders when the Emperor knew the positions of Pacthod and Gérard. Oudinot would guard the neighbourhood of Arcis during the day. Sebastiani to remain where he was, covering the retreat till nightfall, when he would cross and move to Dosnon. It was only at 3 p.m., when he could see the French retreating beyond the river, that Schwarzenberg at last gave the order to advance. The overpowering strength of his artillery soon silenced the French guns, whilst Pahlen defeated the cavalry on their right and took three guns.

Nevertheless, Sebastiani got most of his cavalry over the bridge at Villette, and destroyed it behind him.

In Arcis, Leval's men made a desperate defence from house to house. Attacked on all sides by very superior forces, almost cut from the bridge, they nevertheless succeeded in covering the retreat and destroying the bridge as they passed. The town was clear of French by 6 p.m. Oudinot, with one brigade left in the suburb on the north bank, where Danton once lived, had the rest of his troops at the farther end of the causeway leading through the marshy woods, and at le Chêne. Macdonald reached Ormes with his two divisions at 9 p.m. Gérard could get no farther than Plancy, with Amey's division behind at Anglure. The fords at Plancy and Boulages were watched by two of Macdonald's battalions. Kellermann had joined Sebastiani at Ormes. Macdonald was in great danger, should the allies force the passage, which, fortunately for him, they did not attempt that evening.

As the allies' attack began, Wrede had been ordered to cross the Aube above Chaudrey at Coclois and Ramerupt. Only his cavalry succeeded, the infantry had to go round by Lesmont.

CHAPTER 10

The General Advance on Paris

We have already shown that Napoleon was far from wishing
to fight a great battle at Arcis. It was probably solely owing to
his idea that he had only a rearguard before him that he had advanced on the morning of the 21st. He was at last disillusioned
by the scene which met the eyes of Ney and Sebastiani. He then
knew that there was no chance of his having on that day even
the 50,000 men whom he would have when he was joined by
the whole of Macdonald's army. Even then, he would have a
strength vastly inferior to the 74,000 men whom Schwarzenberg had in front of Arcis, and still more so if we take into consideration the 14,000 still at Troyes and on the Seine. Against
such superiority La Rothière and Laon must have convinced
Napoleon that he had no chance. His estimate of the value of his
personal command was certainly too high. He took, therefore,
the only decision open to him, desperate though it was, to retreat across the river, under the eyes of an enormously superior
enemy, and to make a flank march on Vitry.

He had long meditated a march against Schwarzenberg's rear,
reinforced by the garrisons called up from the fortresses of the
Meuse and the Moselle. He was still intent on it; hence his decision to move on Vitry, and thence, by St. Dizier, up the Marne
towards Schwarzenberg's communications at Chaumont and
Langres. He was of course unaware, on the 20th and the morning of the 21st, of the way in which the right bank of the Aube
had been abandoned by all but the light cavalry of the Russian

Guard. Had he known it by the evening of the 20th, he might have moved towards Brienne by that bank, even without waiting for Macdonald who, as he advanced, could have guarded the Aube against any attempt by Schwarzenberg to cross. Not that any such attempt was likely in the existing state of opinion at allied headquarters. As it was, the Tsar did not approve of Schwarzenberg's bold change of plans, though his disapproval seems curious in view of his previous frequent disapproval of the Austrian's want of enterprise.

Under the circumstances, the probabilities are that, had Schwarzenberg learnt on the 20th that Napoleon was marching on Brienne, he would have at once reversed his engines and hurried off at his best speed to secure his line of retreat by Bar-sur-Aube. Schwarzenberg's failure to attack Arcis on the 21st till he saw clearly that Napoleon was retreating on the Châlons or Vitry roads (they are the same for some distance north of Arcis) was no doubt a grievous error. But Weil makes some excuse for him, on the ground of his personal position as a nominal commander-in-chief, yet obliged to defer to the allied sovereigns, and especially to the Tsar, whose attitude towards him on the previous day had been markedly cold, almost insulting.

Where Weil does find him to blame is in having employed so unnecessarily large a force against Napoleon's rearguard. That, he thinks, could have been easily disposed of by a single corps, the 6th for choice, whilst the rest hurried across the Aube again above Chaudrey, over bridges hastily prepared for them with pontoons, of which the allies always had an ample supply.

Arrived on the right bank in this direction, the allies would have been able, on the 22nd, to act in overwhelming force on the flank of Napoleon's march to Vitry. The Emperor, himself at Sompuis, would have been caught with his army spread out over an immense length, owing to the distance of parts of Macdonald's army, and the necessity of keeping a strong force in front of Arcis and towards Plancy to cover the movement of Macdonald to join him, a movement which could not possibly be completed before the evening of the 22nd. As it was, Schwarzenberg, on the evening of the 21st, was practically out of touch with the enemy, and had no notion whether the Emperor was directing his march on Vitry, on Châlons, or back, by Sézanne, on Paris.

He was not much enlightened on the subject even by the evening of the 22nd. All that day Macdonald's rearguard held on at Arcis and in the neighbourhood with such vigour that the Crown Prince gave up the idea of forcing the passage there, and, under the alternative orders given him by Schwarzenberg, marched the 4th and 6th Corps off across the Aube by Ramerupt to Dampierre. Schwarzenberg had wanted them, after forcing the passages at Arcis, to occupy the line Herbisse-Dosnon; but this was now impossible. The 3rd Corps, so much of it as was up, remained facing Oudinot.

On the evening of the 22nd the 4th Corps stood at Corbeil, the 6th at Dampierre. Kaissarow and Seslawin, on the left of the 3rd Corps, were beating up the country between Méry and Plancy. Wrede, hearing of the confusion and hesitation at headquarters, had stopped his march at Brebant, though his cavalry was pushed forwards towards Vitry. The Guards and Reserves remained behind the Meldançon Brook.

All sorts of contradictory reports added to the confusion at Pougy, where were the Tsar, the king of Prussia, and Schwarzenberg. Wrede averred that Napoleon was moving on Châlons, the Crown Prince named Vitry.

Schwarzenberg proceeded to draft long orders providing for each of three cases, Napoleon's movement on Châlons, on Vitry, or on Montmirail.

Meanwhile, Napoleon had been acting with the utmost vigour. Ney, the Guard, Letort, Berckheim,[1] St. Germain, and Milhaud had all marched on Vitry. The place was strongly held by Colonel von Schwichow with about 5000 Prussians and Russians. Summoned by Ney, he refused to surrender, and some shells thrown into the place had no effect. Ney was, therefore, ordered to mask Vitry and, crossing above it at Frignicourt, to

---

1. Commanding a mixed force of cavalry about 1700 strong, arrived from Paris about the 14th.

push his cavalry on to St. Dizier. At the latter place, Piré with the light cavalry (400 men) captured most of two of the enemy's battalions and a large convoy. There were some other cavalry successes, but, splendid as his dash had been, Piré was not satisfied, complaining that, though Defrance had supported him, St. Germain had stopped at Perthes.

During the night of the 22nd-23rd Macdonald fell back unperceived on Dosnon, whence he marched for Vitry by Trouan and Sommesous, since the enemy's cavalry barred the direct road. His park, in advance of him, was attacked by Osarowski's Guard light cavalry. It should have been guarded by Amey; but that general, under a misapprehension, had gone to meet Pacthod towards Sézanne. Though the drivers and gunners made a brave fight, the whole park would have been carried off but for the timely arrival of Gérard. As it was, fifteen guns and 300 prisoners were carried away, twelve guns spiked, and all the powder destroyed. Thanks to Ney having left Lefol to guard the passage at Frignicourt, Macdonald was able to cross the Marne there on the 23rd before Wrede could arrive, though he had constantly to fight during the day.

Napoleon was between Vitry and St. Dizier on the 22nd, but, having to wait for Macdonald, could only send out cavalry towards Bar-le-Duc, and southwards against Schwarzenberg's communications. On the evening of the 23rd he was with the Guard at St. Dizier, Ney between Vitry and St. Dizier, Macdonald behind him, having just crossed the Marne. Pacthod and Amey, as well as Marmont and Mortier, were now hopelessly cut from Napoleon by the interposition of Schwarzenberg, who stood on the line Soudé Ste. Croix-Courdemanges, with the Guards and Reserves behind the latter, and the 6th and 3rd Corps behind Sompuis.

Meanwhile, allied headquarters at Pougy at first supposed Wrede and the Crown Prince would attack Napoleon, now clearly making for Vitry. But, whilst Schwarzenberg and Radetzky were drawing up orders for the advance on Vitry, there arrived Diebitsch, quartermaster-general of Barclay, bringing intercepted French despatches, including an order from Berthier to Macdonald saying the cavalry was at St. Dizier and Joinville, and requiring him to pass the Marne at once. Before Schwarzenberg had decided what to do, he was summoned to a council of war at Pougy. There he found that news had been received that Pahlen's cavalry was in touch with Winzingerode's advance guard of the Silesian army. Winzingerode already had 8000 cavalry and forty guns at Vitry, and Woronzow with his infantry was on the march from Châlons. Langeron and Sacken were following, whilst Yorck and Kleist were at Château-Thierry, and Billow before Soissons.

Yet another French despatch rider had been taken by Tettenborn. On the prisoner was found a letter from Napoleon to Marie Louise, dated 22nd March, in which it was said,

> On the 21st the enemy drew up in order of battle to protect his march on Brienne and Bar-sur-Aube. I have decided to move on to the Marne, in order to push the enemy's armies farther from Paris, and to draw myself nearer my fortresses.

Another letter to the Empress said,

> The army has passed the Marne near Vitry, and we entered St. Dizier this evening.[2]

There could be no longer any doubt as to the Emperor's movements and intentions. It was, moreover, clear that Napoleon was already so far advanced towards Chaumont that it was no longer possible to prevent his intercepting Schwarzenberg's communications, or even reaching the plateau of Langres.

Were the allies to march after him as he carried away or destroyed all their magazines and depots? If so, it would be hardly possible to stop short of the Rhine; for the army would rapidly become demoralized without supplies in a country where a

---

2. Only copies of these letters were kept by the allies, the originals being made over for delivery to French outposts. The letters are not in the correspondence of Napoleon, but the existence of such letters (the copies are at Vienna) is confirmed by the report of the French officer (at Paris) to whom the originals were made over.

general rising would raise every man's hand against the invader. It does not appear to have struck any one at the council that the obviously correct plan was to advance on Paris with the whole of the armies, leaving Napoleon, at the head of a comparatively small army, to do his worst on the communications with Switzerland. They decided, however, first to unite with the army of Silesia at Châlons, and then with both armies, nearly 200,000 strong, to follow Napoleon.

The communications with Switzerland, being already lost, would be abandoned, and both armies would rely on the line through Laon to the Netherlands. The Emperor of Austria, who was at Bar-sur-Aube, was warned that it was now probably too late for him to rejoin Schwarzenberg, and that he had better make for safety at Dijon with the army of the south. Fortunately, Francis followed the advice, and so saved himself from becoming the prisoner of his son-in-law, whose cavalry were in Bar a few hours after he left.

The idea of marching on Châlons was pure waste of energy and time; for Blücher's advanced guard had already passed it, and to go there only meant a long march which would have to be retraced in following Napoleon. Meanwhile, the appearance of French cavalry at Joinville and other places had already produced the wildest confusion and alarm on the line of communications with Switzerland which continued and increased during the next few days.

Here we must briefly state what had been happening on the northern front since Napoleon, on the 17th March, had left Marmont and Mortier to contain Blücher.

The old field-marshal was still suffering when, on the 18th March, his army at last began to advance again along the Reims road, except Bülow who moved on Soissons. On this day Yorck, supported by a turning movement of Czernitchew's cavalry, forced Ricard from Berry-au-Bac where, however, the French general blew up the bridge.

At this time Mortier was at Reims, with Charpentier's division at Soissons. Marmont, who was in command of the whole, had orders that, if Blücher crossed the Aisne, he was to be checked as much as possible, and Marmont was to cover the road to Paris.[3]

Though the Emperor wrote to him on the 20th to retire on Châlons and Epernay, and censured him later for going by Château-Thierry, [4] it is not very remarkable that, with his existing orders, he should have fallen back on Fismes and called Mortier to join him from Reims. He himself says he took the direction he did in order to cover the Paris road, and to be able to pick up Charpentier.

Marmont was under the impression that Blücher contemplated a general attack on him. That was wrong; for the Prussian was making for Reims and Châlons to rejoin Schwarzenberg. He, therefore, only followed Marmont and Mortier with the corps of Yorck and Kleist. On the 21st the two marshals reached Château-Thierry with Charpentier, who had joined them at Oulchy. In the previous night Marmont had received Napoleon's censure of his march away from Reims and Châlons, with orders to try and regain that road by Epernay; for, without that, Blücher would rejoin Schwarzenberg, and the whole would fall on him (Marmont).[5] Vincent having been driven from Epernay by Tettenborn, Marmont crossed at Château-Thierry, broke down the bridge, and marched on the 22nd towards Etoges. On this day Bülow began bombarding Soissons, and Yorck found himself unable to cross the Marne at Chateau-Thierry.

In the night of the 22nd–23rd Gneisenau diagnosed the position for Blücher thus. [6] The Emperor, he held, had called in Marmont and Mortier and meant to fight with his whole army united. That being so, the army of Silesia should endeavour to fall on Napoleon's flank and rear. Kleist and Yorck were to fol-

---

3. *Corr.* 21,512.

4. *Corr.* 21,522.

5. *Corr.* 21,524.

6. Blücher's appearance at the head of his troops must have been curious; for, refusing to wear goggles or a shade to protect his eyes, he had annexed, from a wardrobe in his quarters, a lady's smart green silk hat, which gave the necessary shade, and wore it for some days. *Weil,* 3. 535

low the marshals; Winzingerode, followed by Sacken and Langeron, by Reims, Epernay, and Châlons on Arcis; Woronzow with Winzingerode's infantry going direct to Châlons.

Though Marmont and Mortier knew that Pacthod and Amey were due, with 4500 men, chiefly National Guards from Paris, at Suzanne, they continued their retreat to Vertus (Marmont) and Etoges (Mortier) on the 23rd.

Napoleon was not altogether displeased with the apparent movements of the allies on the 23rd, for, though the union of their two armies had been facilitated by the direction of Marmont's retreat, they were apparently responding to the Emperor's movement against the communications of the army of Bohemia, by setting out to follow him and abandoning the advance on Paris.

He now, for the moment, gave up the idea of marching on the fortresses, and proposed to seize Bar-sur-Aube and open a new line of operations for himself by Troyes to Paris. On the 23rd he started for Vassy, notwithstanding the fears of Macdonald, who foresaw defeat if he, in his post of rearguard, were attacked, as he expected to be.

That evening Ney was at Vassy, the Guard with Napoleon at Doulevant, Macdonald and Oudinot still at St. Dizier. The cavalry sent towards Bar-le-Duc had been called in, and that in front was already in Colombey-les-deux-Eglises, and knew that Bar-sur-Aube was clear of the enemy. The Emperor's operations on this day (23rd) were unmolested; for, as we know, Schwarzenberg was on his way to Châlons.

During the night of the 23rd-24th much important information reached the allies. There were many reports from the enemies of Napoleon in Paris. Still more important was a despatch from Savary (Minister of Police) taken by Tettenborn's Cossacks. It informed the Emperor that treasury, magazines, and arsenals were equally empty, that the populace, encouraged in disaffection by the enemies of the Empire, was clamouring for peace. Unless Napoleon could draw the allies away from Paris, and avoid returning to the capital himself with the enemy at his heels, there would be an open outbreak.

Schwarzenberg still could not make up his mind to advance on Paris, but he did realize the absurdity of going to Châlons. With the orders and events on the allies' side on the 24th we need not trouble ourselves, except with the all- important, the decisive change in their whole system of operations which, at last, thanks to the Tsar, took place.

Alexander, left alone at Sompuis, whilst Schwarzenberg and the King of Prussia went to arrange for the march on Vitry, sat down to study the captured despatches, especially Savary's. As he read and compared, he realized that Paris, not the Emperor, should now be the objective. Not wishing to be solely responsible, he sent for Barclay, Diebitsch, and Toll. Barclay's opinion was taken first; he was all for following Napoleon. Diebitsch, really in favour of Paris, but not liking to run counter to his chief (Barclay), proposed sending 40,000 or 50,000 men to Paris and following Napoleon with the rest.

Toll, having no ties to Barclay, said plainly that he would like to send only 10,000 cavalry against Napoleon to mask the movement of the rest of the united armies on Paris. That fitted in precisely with Alexander's views, which he had hitherto kept to himself. To Diebitsch's remark that the march on Paris implied a restoration of the Bourbons, the Tsar replied shortly, "There is no question of the Bourbons; it is a question of overturning Napoleon."

Nor did he give any weight to Barclay's argument that Napoleon would reach Paris before them, or to his inferences based on what had happened at Moscow in 1812. Diebitsch, too, now seeing how the wind blew, went over to Alexander's side. Then they all went off after the King of Prussia and Schwarzenberg. Frederick William, as usual, agreed with the Tsar, and Schwarzenberg had no option but to accept the proposal, which was that, next day, the 6th Corps should march on Fère Champenoise, followed by the 4th, the cavalry of both acting as advanced guard. The Guards and Reserves to follow by Sompuis and Mailly; Wrede to march by the high-road; the 3rd Ccorps to march on Fère Champenoise from the place where it received the orders; Kaissarow to stay at Arcis, maintaining communication with Troyes.

As it was not known exactly where Blücher was, orders were sent direct to Winzingerode to follow Napoleon with his cavalry, and to send Czernitchew's Cossacks to Montier-en-Der to watch the country between the Marne and Aube; Tettenborn to watch towards Metz, in case the enemy should undertake anything in that direction. Woronzow was to march, on the 25th, from Châlons to Etoges; Langeron and Sacken to join him.

The new direction was communicated to Blücher, who was told to try and take Soissons and hold it. Needless to say, Blücher received the news with delight. "I was sure," he exclaimed, "my brave brother Schwarzenberg would be of the same opinion as myself. Now we shall soon be done with the business." [7]

He alone of the allied commanders had correctly gauged Napoleon's movement as a last desperate effort to draw the allies from Paris, in which the fortunes of his empire were centred. Some of the others thought he meant to make his last fight beyond the Rhine; others that he would make for the Netherlands, defeat or gain over Bernadotte, and then return, reinforced by the garrisons, against the allied armies. Blücher, even before he heard of the decision of Sompuis, had ordered Sacken towards Paris by Montmirail. He planned a concentration of his army at Meaux on the 28th, the very day on which headquarters had now resolved to unite both armies there for the final march on Paris.

Here, in order to get a clear view of the situation of affairs, we summarize the positions of both sides in the night of the 24th. On the allied side, the army of Bohemia stood west of Vitry, ready to move westwards, except the 3rd corps which was north of Mailly on the Arcis-Châlons road. Winzingerode was on the right bank of the Marne with his cavalry between Vitry and St. Dizier. Sacken, Woronzow, and Langeron were about Châlons, under orders to march by the Montmirail road. Kleist and Yorck

---

7. Varnhagen-von-Ense, *Life of Blücher*, 427.

were between Château-Thierry and Montmirail; Bülow before Soissons.

On the French side, Macdonald was still at St. Dizier, Ney at Vassy, Napoleon and the Guard at Doulevant, with Pire's cavalry towards Chaumont, and St. Germain's towards Bar-sur-Aube. All these were safe from immediate serious molestation, but it was otherwise with the remaining French corps. Marmont was at Soudé Ste. Croix, waiting for Mortier marching from Vertus. Both were trying to join the Emperor by Vitry, but were hopelessly cut from him by four allied corps in front, and the 3rd Corps and Seslawin on Marmont's right rear. Pacthod and Amey were at Vertus, between the three corps of Sacken, Langeron, and Woronzow at Châlons, and the corps of Yorck and Kleist approaching Montmirail. Compans was at Sézanne with the scattered detachments which he had been ordered to collect there. His retreat was still open by La Ferté Gaucher and Meaux.

Schwarzenberg's orders for the 25th arrived too late for an early start, but by 8 a.m. Pahlen's 3600 cavalry found Marmont drawn up at Soude Ste. Croix. The French retired in good order, and were presently joined by Mortier. The Crown Prince of Würtemberg decided to attack without waiting for his infantry. His cavalry was gradually reinforced till, at 4 p.m., he had at least 12,000. [8] The French cavalry behaved badly, and Marmont and Mortier, driven from position to position, often in disorder, had only effected their escape through Fère Champenoise to Allemant when the Crown Prince decided to wait for infantry, which could not be up till next morning.

At one time, the French, hearing artillery fire from the northeast, were cheered with the belief that the Emperor was coming to their assistance. But what they heard was something quite different. Marmont and Mortier lost this day 2000 killed and wounded, 4000 prisoners, 45 guns, and 100 ammunition wagons, out of a total strength of 19,000 men. [9]

What they had heard in the north-east was the last gallant fight

8. Houssaye says 20,000.
9. Houssaye says only 16,580.

of Pacthod and Amey who, with 4300 men and sixteen guns, guarding a large convoy of food and ammunition, had spent the night at Bergeres and were on the march to Vatry, where they hoped to meet Mortier. They had halted at Villeséneux to eat when they were attacked by Korff with Langeron's cavalry and Karpow's Cossacks. They had reached Clamanges on the way to Fère Champenoise, retiring from position to position in squares, when Pacthod saw it was necessary to abandon the convoy.

Between 2 and 3 p.m. Pacthod was at Ecury-le-Repos when fresh hostile cavalry began to sweep down on the little force from every direction: Wassiltchikow from the north with Sacken's cavalry; Pahlen's cavalry from the south-west, sent back by the Crown Prince to see what was happening on his right rear; from the south thirty Russian guns, brought up by the Tsar himself, fired on the French squares. The National Guards, who formed the bulk of the French, fought like veterans.

It was only when his squares were broken and Pacthod himself wounded that he was forced to surrender. Amey, too, his troops in a single square, trying to get away into the great marsh of St. Gond, was surrounded by cavalry. Still the French would not surrender. Nearly every man was killed, wounded or captured, and only a very few succeeded in escaping to the marshes.

The total loss of Marmont, Mortier, Pacthod, and Amey was some 10,000 men and over sixty guns. The allies only lost 2000 men.

For Napoleon, the 25th March had been a day of uncertainty and hesitation. From his lieutenants there came in the most contradictory and perplexing reports of the enemy's movements, most of them wrong either in their facts, or their inferences, or both. Piré with the cavalry southwards continued to report the spread of panic on the lines of communication of the army of Bohemia. During the day he occupied Chaumont, and heard of preparations for evacuating Langres. News came in that Troyes was being evacuated, and that the Emperor of Austria had fled to Dijon.

In the opposite direction, Schwarzenberg appeared to have

stopped his advance on Vitry, or at least not to be pressing it. Macdonald had not been molested as he marched from St. Dizier. Ney reported all quiet towards Vitry, but that the allies seemed to be marching for Brienne. If the allied commander-in-chief had been any one but Schwarzenberg, the advance on Paris might have been suspected; but such a resolution could hardly be believed, looking to what had happened hitherto.

At 3.30 a.m. Napoleon wrote to Berthier that it would be four or five hours before he could have clear ideas as to what the enemy was doing.[10] He ordered his corps to halt where they were. In the afternoon, Macdonald reported artillery fire against his rearguard, Ney that 10,000 cavalry, coming from Vitry, were arriving at St. Dizier. There was nothing to show whether this large cavalry body was the advanced guard of a great army advancing on St. Dizier, or only a detached force.

Anyhow, there was a good opportunity to overwhelm it. Macdonald was on the left bank of the Marne now, but the river was fordable here in many places. At 9 p.m. orders issued for the morrow. The Emperor proposed to attack this force and drive it against the Marne. The enemy was scattered (so Napoleon thought), and there was every chance of a good day's work.

Nevertheless, the Emperor's confidence had deserted him. Two days before, when Caulaincourt, returning after the breaking off of the Châtillon negotiations, had urged an attempt to reopen them, Napoleon would have nothing to do with it. Now he authorized his plenipotentiary to follow the course he had proposed. Moreover, he agreed to give up a frontier extending to the left bank of the Rhine. But the possibility of a renewal of negotiations did not turn him from his projects of battle.

By dawn on the 26th Napoleon was at Vassy where he learnt, from Macdonald, that only a few Cossacks were now in contact with him. These Cossacks, under Tettenborn, forming Winzingerode's advanced guard, were easily driven across the Marne, and from the heights on the left bank the Emperor plainly saw the whole of Winzingerode's mass of cavalry drawn up in two

10. *Corr.* 21,541.

lines, the first on the hither side, the second on the farther side of the Vitry-St. Dizier road. Their left rested on St. Dizier, defended by 1000 infantry, their right on the warren of Perthes, the edge of which was also held by a battalion. There were skirmishers along the river.

The advance began at once, Oudinot moving on St. Dizier, the whole of the cavalry, headed by Sebastiani, crossing a ford below the town, followed by Macdonald, Gérard, and the Old Guard. The cavalry, first driving in Tettenborn's Cossacks, advanced against the enemy's centre. The Russians began to give way at once, and Winzingerode ordered Tettenborn to retire on Vitry, whilst he himself fell back on Bar-le-Duc, endeavouring to take with him the infantry in St. Dizier. As the enemy's cavalry formed column of march, Sebastiani sent against their flank the dragoons of the Guard and the mounted grenadiers, supported by the 2000 dragoons from Spain under Treilliard.

The broken horsemen of Winzingerode fled, partly towards Bar-le-Duc, partly into the forest north of St. Dizier. The former line was taken also by the infantry from St. Dizier. They were soon caught by Treilliard, who cut them down and pursued them two-thirds of the way to Bar-le-Duc.

On the other side L'Héritier's cavalry division drove Tettenborn and the skirmishers towards Perthes.

Winzingerode had, in a couple of hours, been driven completely from his position in two directions, with a loss of 1500 men and nine guns. [11]

The victory, such as it was, was Napoleon's last, except Ligny in 1815. It did not bring much relief to his difficulties. It did not go far to show him what the allies were really doing, but it was pretty clear evidence that Winzingerode's cavalry was not the strong advanced guard of a great army; for it was clearly unsupported.

Napoleon's uneasiness was added to by the statements of prisoners that the main army was marching on Paris. Still, such statements were not enough to go upon; for the Emperor him-

11. According to Weil. Houssaye puts the loss higher,.

self had only recently ordered his commanders to spread reports among their men that his march was on Metz, whilst it was really on Bar-sur-Aube. This had been done with the deliberate intention of preventing prisoners giving true information. [12]

Napoleon, no doubt, had begun to suspect the truth on the evening of the 26th, and it was with a view to enlightenment that he ordered Oudinot to push next day on Bar-le-Duc, whilst he himself marched for Vitry.

In the afternoon of the 27th, when he was before Vitry, news came in from all directions, including intercepted despatches and proclamations of the allies, which placed the question beyond the possibility of doubt.

What was he to do now in this most critical period of his affairs? Should he return by forced marches on Paris? The enemy had gained three days' march on him, and the probabilities were that he would find them already in occupation of the capital, the defences of which had been sadly neglected.

He had often, during the earlier part of the campaign, asserted that he could not afford to lose Paris, but latterly he had said that he had not ceased "to foresee this eventuality, and had familiarized himself with the decisions which it would entail." [13] If he remained in the east and let Paris go, he would be joined shortly by Durutte from Metz with 4000 men, besides what might be collected from Longwy, Montmédy, Luxemburg, and Sarrelouis. Broussier with 5000 men was about to break out of Strasburg, collecting the garrisons in that direction; 2000 men from Verdun were on the march to Châlons; Souham's division from Nogent-sur-Seine, and Allix's 2000 from Auxerre might be drawn in. In addition to all these, the whole countryside was arming, or clamouring for arms.

On the other hand, there was to be reckoned with the discontent of his commanders, knowing that their homes in Paris were abandoned to the enemy, and that the war, once transferred to Alsace and Lorraine, might last indefinitely. In the end, the

12. Houssaye, 391.
13. Fain, 203.

Emperor yielded to these latter considerations. At 11 p.m. on the 27th, orders issued for the march of the army on Paris by the longer but clearer route by Bar-sur-Aube, Troyes, and Fontainebleau.

In the morning of the 28th, as Napoleon was leaving St. Dizier, Count Weissenberg, the Austrian ambassador to England, was brought in a prisoner. Him Napoleon sent off to negotiate with the Austrian Emperor, just as he had sent Meerveldt during the battle of Leipzig. Caulaincourt also wrote to Metternich.

At Doulevant, in the evening of the 28th, the Emperor received an urgent call for his presence in Paris, which the allies were approaching. He was obliged to sleep at Doulevant, for his army had not advanced far enough to make it safe for him, with a small escort, to go ahead of it. On the 29th, at Dolancourt, he heard that the allies were in possession of Meaux, and that fighting was already going on at Claye, only fifteen miles from Paris. The troops were hurried on at lightning speed, and Troyes was reached that night. The Guard marched forty-three miles that day.

At daybreak on the 30th the Emperor started ahead, leaving Berthier in command, with orders to hurry on. At first he rode with an escort of two squadrons. Then he began to think that by driving he might reach Paris that night. He, with Caulaincourt, set out from Villeneuve l'Archevêque in a light wicker carriage, followed by Drouot and Flahault in another, and by Gourgaud and Marshal Lefebvre in a third. The last-named, as one of the people, would be useful in organizing a defence by the working classes.

As he drove in his wretched conveyance, bad news poured in upon the Emperor. At Sens he heard that the enemy was before Paris; at Fontainebleau that the Empress was gone from Paris, a move which he could not justly blame, for he himself had ordered it, if she and her son were in danger of capture by the allies. At Essonne he heard that a battle was raging before Paris.

He had reached the post-house of La Cour de France, only twelve miles from Paris, and was impatiently awaiting a change of horses, when there arrived a body of cavalry, under Belliard. In reply to the Emperor's storm of questions, Belliard told him of the battle of Paris, and of the convention about to be signed, under which Marmont was to evacuate the capital next morning. Still Napoleon insisted on making for Paris, and had actually gone a mile or two on the road when he found himself in view of the enemy's bivouac fires barring the road. Unable to go farther, he returned to La Cour de France. Flahault was sent off to urge Marmont to hold out. At the same time, Caulaincourt was despatched to Paris with full powers to conclude peace, in the vain hope that negotiations might still be possible.

A very few words must suffice to describe what had happened as the allies advanced on Paris after the defeat of Marmont, Mortier, Pacthod, and Amey on the 25th.

The two marshals, reaching Sézanne on the 26th, found part of Yorck's and Kleist's corps already there. Compelled to turn southwards, as the road to Meaux was barred, they marched hard for Paris by Provins, and succeeded in reaching the capital unmolested on the 29th.

Compans had been just in time to get away from Sézanne to Meaux, where he picked up some reinforcements of small military value. He was driven from Meaux to Claye, where he met another 3400 reinforcements. He made one or two more attempts to stand between Meaux and Paris, before which he arrived on the 29th.

In the evening of the 29th the allies were in front of the capital, on its eastern and northern sides, with 107,000 men. Sacken and Wrede had been left about Trilport to meet a possible attack by Napoleon; Bülow was besieging Soissons; Winzingerode's cavalry was still towards Montier-en-Der. Napoleon's own army was still almost entirely east of Troyes. Opposed to the army in front of Paris, Marmont had nearly 12,000 regular troops, Mortier about 11,000, and Moncey the garrison of Paris, mostly National Guards, raising the total to about 42,000 troops, good, bad, and in different, with 154 guns.

Very little had been done towards fortifying the capital. It is easy to understand that, though Napoleon had talked of making Paris a strong place, it was with reluctance that he viewed operations which would tend to make the people think that he, the conqueror of Europe, had to look to earthworks for the defence of his capital. When, therefore, Joseph sent him projects for fortifications, he sometimes said they required further consideration, some- times neglected to supply the necessary funds, sometimes did not answer at all.

Beyond the incomplete "*octroi*" wall, and a few trenches, batteries, redoubts, and barricades, Paris was unfortified when the allies attacked on the 30th March.

Of the battle of Paris we do not propose to give any detailed account. By 4 p.m. the French had been driven back to the heights of Belleville on the right (Marmont), and Montmartre on the left (Mortier) with a connecting line between.

The Emperor, as we know, was then hurrying by Fontainebleau in his wicker carriage. Of his own army, Souham was at Nogent-sur-Seine, the Guard at Villeneuve l'Archevêque, Ney at Troyes, Macdonald between Vendœuvre and Troyes, Piré on the Aube.

With the negotiations between Marmont and the allies in the evening and night of the 30th, with the capitulation of Paris, or with the subsequent negotiations which led to the first abdication of Napoleon and his departure for Elba, we do not propose to deal. They are fully narrated in many non-military histories, and in the admirable *1814* of the late M. Henry Houssaye, a book equally excellent from a military and from a political point of view, one which is deficient only in the absence of good maps to illustrate the progress of military events.

Clausewitz has poured scorn on Napoleon's attempt to draw the allies from Paris by a march against Schwarzenberg's communications, treating it as a mere gambler's desperate throw. On general principles, no doubt, the move should have proved, as it did prove, futile. But, looking to the special circumstances of the case, and to the personality of Schwarzenberg, was it so bound to fail as Clausewitz thinks? The whole of Schwarzenberg's conduct in 1813 and 1814, his almost insane nervousness regarding his communications, surely gave the Emperor good reason to believe that such a manoeuvre, the fear of which had already induced the Austrian commander-in-chief to abandon the march on Paris rather than risk having his communications cut, would succeed once more.

As a matter of fact, it had succeeded on the 23rd March in deciding the council of war of Pougy to vote for following Napoleon, rather than risk the move on Paris. It was only on the 25th that the Tsar, to whom the whole credit is due, compelled a change of plan and a determined advance on Paris. Even he, perhaps, would not have been bold enough to advocate this course but for Savary's letter to the Emperor, which fortune had placed in his hands, and the correctness of the contents of which was confirmed by reports from friends in Paris. Napoleon's move was, no doubt, a desperate one, but it was the last open to him, and, looking to all the circumstances, it may well be doubted whether it was quite so absurd as Clausewitz seems to think. For once, it looks as if the great critic had allowed his judgment to be warped by the actual result.

CHAPTER 11

Concluding Remarks

Before closing this account of Napoleon's penultimate campaign, it may be well to glance back briefly at its principal features, and the lessons which they teach. The campaign of 1814 has been greatly admired, and has even been held up as the greatest effort of the Emperor's genius.

If, on the one hand, we think this estimate places it too high, on the other, it is certainly a wonderful example of what Napoleon's genius could do in circumstances which, since the great defeat of Leipzig, had become so desperate that no other general of the time would have even attempted to make head against them. To find a parallel we have to go back to Frederick the Great in his struggle against almost all the rest of Europe.

Napoleon had lost practically the whole of the great army of 1812, and that had been replaced in 1813 by another of inferior quality, which he had conjured up as if by magic. Now that, too, had nearly disappeared, except for the garrisons left behind in the German fortresses. For Napoleon these were as much lost as the dead, disabled, and prisoners of Lützen, Bautzen, Dresden, and Leipzig.

But the spirit of the great leader was still unquelled, though he found it impossible to raise from exhausted and discontented France the new troops he wanted. Time was his most urgent need, and the allies seemed determined to give him that, by delaying their advance and negotiating for a peace which, perhaps, they never intended to grant, or Napoleon to accept.

Still, the Emperor had not sufficient time; for he was bound to Paris by the immense labours of organization and of government, which he alone could control. When, at last, he tore himself away to return to the front at Châlons, he was a week too late to be able to fall upon one of the allied armies, Blücher's for choice, before they could unite.

Their union had been effected, though it was still by no means complete, and there was yet a chance of inflicting a heavy blow on Blücher before he was fully supported by the slow-moving corps of the army of Bohemia. Napoleon's attack on Blücher at Brienne was the most natural course for him to take; but it failed, and henceforward he must have known that he had to reckon also with a large part of Schwarzenberg's army. Here he made his first great mistake, in waiting too long about Brienne, until he could not avoid the battle of La Rothière in which, with his inferior numbers and poor position, he could not reasonably hope for success.

He was saved from complete ruin by the faults of the allies, which were numerous. Forgetting that it is never possible to be too strong on the decisive battle- field, Schwarzenberg wasted Wittgenstein's corps, and perhaps Yorck's also. Even Wrede would have been sent off after Wittgenstein, but for his own suggestion crossing Schwarzenberg's orders. The limitations of Blücher's command were bound, as for political reasons they were intended, to prevent the realization of the full fruits of victory. Blücher himself failed to perceive that Napoleon's left, not his centre, was the point on which the main effort was required. His own centre, with the Guards and Reserves behind it, was safe from any counter-attack Napoleon could make on it.

The pursuit on the 2nd February was tardy and inefficient, and another great mistake was made in the separation of the armies of Silesia and Bohemia. As has already been pointed out, Blücher, at this time, had no prospects of reinforcement to a strength much exceeding 50,000 men, a number which would not give him any marked superiority to the force Napoleon would be able to bring against him.

Napoleon, having failed to cut off Blücher as he had hoped, had now to recommence that system of "*va et vient* " marching alternately against each of the hostile armies, of which he was so great a master. For his purpose of containing one enemy with a portion of his force, whilst he fell on the other with the rest, the river system of Champagne was of the greatest advantage. The Seine and its tributaries in particular facilitated defence against an enemy advancing on that side.

The main road by which Schwarzenberg was advancing from the plateau of Langres had first to pass the Aube at Bar-sur-Aube. Then it met the Seine at Troyes where a defence was possible. The great northward bend of the river between Troyes and Montereau necessitated a second passage of the river at Nogent or Bray. Schwarzenberg could in this part only advance on the south bank; for the roads on the north bank were bad, and moreover the Aube had to be crossed. Moreover, any attempt to pass round the bend would expose the allies to attack in left flank by Napoleon holding the passages of the Seine.

Below Nogent Schwarzenberg could move by both banks, but his force on the south bank would encounter the lines of the Yonne and the Loing. Moreover, the French, destroying the bridges of the Seine as they passed, and leaving others intact behind them, might at any moment attack the enemy on one bank with strong forces, leaving only a weak one to contain him on the opposite bank.

The Marne, too, was a good line for the defence of Paris. The main road from Germany to Paris crossed it at Châlons, at Château-Thierry, at La Ferté-sous-Jouarre, and yet again at Trilport.

Napoleon's movement against Blücher in the second and third weeks of February was, as we have said, his most successful manoeuvre of this campaign; but we have also endeavoured to show that much of its success was due to fortuitous circumstances, and to Schwarzenberg's removal of the connecting link between the two armies, without informing Blücher. Both the prescience often attributed to Napoleon, and the incapacity alleged to have been displayed by Blücher in disseminating his forces require to be discounted considerably. Napoleon had no certain knowledge of the dispersion of the army of Silesia until he reached Sézanne. Blücher's great faults were, first, in not keeping in better touch with Seslawin's movements, and secondly, in trying to combine two incompatible objectives at the same time, namely, the rallying of Kleist and Kapzewitch, and the pursuit and envelopment of Macdonald. The first fault was one of constant occurrence in the allied armies and was, perhaps, inherent in a divided command.

It is hardly possible to give too much credit to the leaders and troops of the Silesian army for the wonderful way in which they pulled themselves together at Châlons after the very severe handling they had had.

When Napoleon, having beaten but by no means destroyed Blücher, returned to his containing force on the Seine, he decided to meet the enemy in front, not to march against his right flank and rear, as he did in the latter part of March. His strength, combined with that of the containing force, was little more than half that of the army of Bohemia. The proportion of forces was generally the same throughout the campaign, and consequently the Emperor was never able to provide a reasonably large containing force, and at the same time to carry with himself an army even equal in numbers to the hostile army against which he moved offensively. He had to rely largely on the real value and the prestige of his personal presence at the head of troops.

The success of his movement against Schwarzenberg, in the second half of February, was, as he complained bitterly, marred by his want of the means of passing the Seine at Nogent, in pursuit of the enemy. Had he been able to do so, it might well have gone hard with Schwarzenberg's advanced left wing. As it was, Napoleon owed a debt of gratitude to Pajol for his brilliant cavalry action at Montereau, which secured for the Emperor the bridges over the Seine and Yonne at their junction.

When Schwarzenberg got back to Troyes, he was in a difficult position for a leader of his character. The country in which he stood was poor at the best, and now its resources were exhausted. Napoleon, on the other hand, had at his back the richer country towards Paris. Schwarzenberg, therefore, must either fight a decisive battle or must fall back to Langres. He would dearly have loved to return to the eighteenth-century system of manoeuvring, but that was not possible with an adversary like Napoleon, or in an exhausted country.

There cannot be a shadow of a doubt that, from a military point of view, Schwarzenberg should have fought a great battle, in which, with Blücher to help him, he could have opposed the Emperor with more than twofold forces. He appears to have made up his mind to fight until the news of Augereau's advance from the south alarmed him for his communications with Switzerland, and decided him in favour of a retreat towards the plateau of Langres, and a fresh separation from Blücher. He also weakened his own army by the despatch of Bianchi and a large force to Dijon.

Napoleon had hoped for a battle about Troyes, though, as we have seen, his chances of success in it were small. We have already commented on his apparent reluctance to believe that Blücher was again marching on Paris, until the Prussian had already gained a considerable start of him. Still, Napoleon kept his main body at Troyes ready for all eventualities, either to support the pursuit of Schwarzenberg or to follow Blücher, according to circumstances.

Marmont and Mortier (the former was chiefly responsible) deserve great credit for their little campaign on the Lower Ourcq, during the period before the Emperor reached La Ferté-sous-Jouarre, and during his detention there, owing to his want of the means of throwing bridges. Nevertheless, Blücher succeeded in escaping across the Upper Ourcq, and it may be said that when Napoleon at last crossed the Marne on the 3rd March, he had practically lost all chance of compelling Blücher to fight before he was joined by Winzingerode and by Bülow. Of the latter's whereabouts Napoleon was in complete ignorance.

It may be thought that the Emperor would have done better,

instead of waiting for the repair of the bridge at La Ferté-sous-Jouarre, to have marched direct to Château-Thierry, and crossed there as Victor actually did. But he could feel no certainty that he would not find the same difficulty in crossing at Château-Thierry that he had already found at La Ferté-sous-Jouarre. Moreover, he must have felt nervous as to the period during which Marmont and Mortier could maintain themselves on the Ourcq, and prevent Blücher's march on Paris.

Lastly, the roads to Château-Thierry were very bad, as he knew from experience three weeks earlier. Once Blücher had been reinforced by Winzingerode and Bülow, his strength was more than double that of Napoleon, who could hardly hope for success in a battle against such odds. What happened at Craonne and Laon we know, and the Emperor probably owed his escape from ruin after the latter battle largely to Blücher's physical breakdown.

The march on Reims, and the defeat of St. Priest were very brilliant affairs in Napoleon's best style, and had important political results in restoring the Emperor's fading prestige in Paris, as well as the military result of again severing all direct communication between Blücher and Schwarzenberg.

Having just dealt with the movement on Arcis and against Schwarzenberg's communications, we need not refer further to the subject.

We have not said much of Napoleon's attempts to harass the allies by raising the country against them. But for the conduct of some of the allied troops themselves, especially the Cossacks, it seems probable that the Emperor would have had little chance of raising the country people to armed resistance. They were tired of the years of war, which had carried off their sons and husbands to supply the constant demand for conscripts, and they would no doubt have watched almost with indifference the progress of an invasion conducted with humanity. But the atrocities of the Cossacks and others, though they were little, if at all, worse than those committed in the past by French troops in Germany, exasperated the inhabitants, and prepared them to respond in desperation to the Emperor's calls to rise and defend themselves. There were frequent encounters with armed peasants, and many stragglers of the allies, or small parties, were cut off, and either massacred or captured. Convoys were also cut off, if not strongly guarded.

In this way the allies were undoubtedly hampered, and compelled, as Napoleon had been compelled in 1813, to take special precautions. But it cannot be said that the general course of the war was seriously influenced by popular risings.

As for the negotiations, which commenced from Frankfort in November, 1813, and continued off and on till the middle of March, 1814, it is difficult to believe that either side was in earnest. On the whole, it is more probable that the allies, with the divergent views and aims of their different groups, would have welcomed peace than that Napoleon would have accepted terms which, if they were to lead to permanent peace, would have shorn him of all his conquests, and put an end to his dreams of universal empire. Generally speaking, he was only open to reason when affairs were going badly with him.

A success, such as that against Blücher in the middle of February, or the subsequent victories over Schwarzenberg, at once raised his hopes and his terms, and set him definitely against peace. Caulaincourt, who saw more clearly that in peace lay the only chance of recovery, was unable to influence his Imperial and imperious master. In this campaign Napoleon's insane optimism constantly blinded him to actual facts, even more than was the case in 1813. It seems almost as if he believed that the fall of the conqueror of Europe was an unthinkable contingency.

Weather played an important part in this campaign. Continued alternations of frost and thaw rendered the roads almost unpassable, and the rivers unfordable everywhere. On the whole, probably, this was an advantage to Napoleon; for the wonderful marching powers of even French recruits gave him an advantage over the slower moving allies. This advantage was increased by the fact that Napoleon, operating in his own country, was generally able, as before Champaubert, to get willing help from the peasantry and their farm horses in dragging his guns over roads which it seemed almost impossible for them to traverse, as well as in food supplies.

It has been said that Napoleon's great want in 1813 and 1814 was cavalry. Yet, in the latter year, it may be remarked that he was often proportionately stronger in cavalry than his enemies, whose total numbers throughout were generally double his. When he marched against Blücher on the 9th February, one-third of his force was cavalry, an arm in which Blücher at the moment was weak.

It must be admitted that much of the French cavalry was of the poorest description: that many of the recruits had never been on a horse till a fortnight before their first battle, that they could only just hold their reins in one hand and a sword in the other, and that both hands had to be used when they wanted to turn their horses. Still, the Emperor had some good cavalry, especially the cavalry of the Guard, and the squadrons of Treilliard and Sparre, veterans of the war in Spain. What his cavalry was still capable of under his command was seen at Vauchamps. If Sebastiani's troopers yielded to panic at Arcis in the morning of the 20th March, they nobly redeemed their reputation in the charge of the same night.

The artillery, too, was of very varied quality, some of it atrociously bad and untrained, some of it, especially the famous artillery of the Guard, as good as ever. In this arm Napoleon's most powerful enemy was the Russian artillery, which, always good and well led, made it a point of honour not to lose guns.

The French infantry ranged in quality from the splendid veterans of Spain and of the Old Guard to the poor recruits of Pacthod's National Guards, and some even less trained. Yet even these covered themselves with glory, and died fighting to the last, in the bloody actions near Fère Champenoise.

When all was over, both Napoleon and his troops might well have said, with François I. after Pavia, "*Tout est perdu fors l'honneur.*"

LEONAUR

ALSO FROM LEONAUR
AVAILABLE IN SOFTCOVER OR HARDCOVER WITH DUST JACKET

CAPTAIN OF THE 95th (Rifles) *by Jonathan Leach*—An officer of Wellington's Sharpshooters during the Peninsular, South of France and Waterloo Campaigns of the Napoleonic Wars.

BUGLER AND OFFICER OF THE RIFLES *by William Green & Harry Smith* With the 95th (Rifles) during the Peninsular & Waterloo Campaigns of the Napoleonic Wars

BAYONETS, BUGLES AND BONNETS *by James 'Thomas' Todd*—Experiences of hard soldiering with the 71st Foot - the Highland Light Infantry - through many battles of the Napoleonic wars including the Peninsular & Waterloo Campaigns

THE ADVENTURES OF A LIGHT DRAGOON *by George Farmer & G.R. Gleig*—A cavalryman during the Peninsular & Waterloo Campaigns, in captivity & at the siege of Bhurtpore, India

THE COMPLEAT RIFLEMAN HARRIS *by Benjamin Harris as told to & transcribed by Captain Henry Curling*—The adventures of a soldier of the 95th (Rifles) during the Peninsular Campaign of the Napoleonic Wars

WITH WELLINGTON'S LIGHT CAVALRY *by William Tomkinson*—The Experiences of an officer of the 16th Light Dragoons in the Peninsular and Waterloo campaigns of the Napoleonic Wars.

SURTEES OF THE RIFLES *by William Surtees*—A Soldier of the 95th (Rifles) in the Peninsular campaign of the Napoleonic Wars.

ENSIGN BELL IN THE PENINSULAR WAR *by George Bell*—The Experiences of a young British Soldier of the 34th Regiment 'The Cumberland Gentlemen' in the Napoleonic wars.

WITH THE LIGHT DIVISION *by John H. Cooke*—The Experiences of an Officer of the 43rd Light Infantry in the Peninsula and South of France During the Napoleonic Wars

NAPOLEON'S IMPERIAL GUARD: FROM MARENGO TO WATERLOO *by J. T. Headley*—This is the story of Napoleon's Imperial Guard from the bearskin caps of the grenadiers to the flamboyance of their mounted chasseurs, their principal characters and the men who commanded them.

BATTLES & SIEGES OF THE PENINSULAR WAR *by W. H. Fitchett*—Corunna, Busaco, Albuera, Ciudad Rodrigo, Badajos, Salamanca, San Sebastian & Others

LEONAUR

ALSO FROM LEONAUR

AVAILABLE IN SOFTCOVER OR HARDCOVER WITH DUST JACKET

WELLINGTON AND THE PYRENEES CAMPAIGN VOLUME I: FROM VI-TORIA TO THE BIDASSOA *by F. C. Beatson*—The final phase of the campaign in the Iberian Peninsula.

WELLINGTON AND THE INVASION OF FRANCE VOLUME II: THE BIDAS-SOA TO THE BATTLE OF THE NIVELLE *by F. C. Beatson*—The second of Beatson's series on the fall of Revolutionary France published by Leonaur, the reader is once again taken into the centre of Wellington's strategic and tactical genius.

WELLINGTON AND THE FALL OF FRANCE VOLUME III: THE GAVES AND THE BATTLE OF ORTHEZ *by F. C. Beatson*—This final chapter of F. C. Beatson's brilliant trilogy shows the 'captain of the age' at his most inspired and makes all three books essential additions to any Peninsular War library.

NAVAL BATTLES OF THE NAPOLEONIC WARS *by W. H. Fitchett*—Cape St. Vincent, the Nile, Cadiz, Copenhagen, Trafalgar & Others

SERGEANT GUILLEMARD: THE MAN WHO SHOT NELSON? *by Robert Guillemard*—A Soldier of the Infantry of the French Army of Napoleon on Campaign Throughout Europe

WITH THE GUARDS ACROSS THE PYRENEES *by Robert Batty*—The Experiences of a British Officer of Wellington's Army During the Battles for the Fall of Napoleonic France, 1813.

A STAFF OFFICER IN THE PENINSULA *by E. W. Buckham*—An Officer of the British Staff Corps Cavalry During the Peninsula Campaign of the Napoleonic Wars

THE LEIPZIG CAMPAIGN: 1813—NAPOLEON AND THE "BATTLE OF THE NATIONS" *by F. N. Maude*—Colonel Maude's analysis of Napoleon's campaign of 1813.

BUGEAUD: A PACK WITH A BATON by *Thomas Robert Bugeaud*—The Early Campaigns of a Soldier of Napoleon's Army Who Would Become a Marshal of France.

TWO LEONAUR ORIGINALS

SERGEANT NICOL by *Daniel Nicol*—The Experiences of a Gordon Highlander During the Napoleonic Wars in Egypt, the Peninsula and France.

WATERLOO RECOLLECTIONS by *Frederick Llewellyn*—Rare First Hand Accounts, Letters, Reports and Retellings from the Campaign of 1815.

CPSIA information can be obtained at www.ICGtesting.com
Printed in the USA
BVOW08s0020290715

410876BV00001B/101/P